The problem with the world is that everyone is a few drinks behind.

Humphrey Bogart

Thanks for dining with us at Va de Vi

KAYU N!O
We liked u!

Loved the
food — LOVED the
wine!!!

XO, T.T.M & B :)

Cheers!
Cheers.
greats George & I definately had a good meal here worthy of note.
Ken

THANKS!
HEY RICHIE!!

D0099485

Va de Vi

BISTRO · WINE BAR

The Va de Vi

Cookbook

Dale Raaen with Kelly Degala and Brendan Eliason
Foreword by Marlene Sorosky Gray

The Va de Vi Cookbook
Text, photography, and illustrations copyright © 2006 by Raaen Walz Management LLC
1511 Mt. Diablo Boulevard

Walnut Creek, CA 94596

All rights reserved. No part of this publication may be reproduced in any form or by any means, electronic or mechanical, including photocopying and recording, or by any information storage and retrieval system, without prior written permission from Favorite Recipes Press.

Manufactured by

Favorite Recipes® Press

P.O. Box 305142

Nashville, Tennessee 37230

800-358-0560

The Va de Vi Cookbook written by: Dale Raaen with Kelly Degala and Brendan Eliason; foreword by Marlene Sorosky Gray

Recipes by: Kelly Degala

Recipe consultant: Marlene Sorosky Gray

Photography by: David Broach and Audrey Dempsey

Book designed by: JoAnn Tracht-Rawson with Bob Dempsey

ISBN 0-9772153-0-X

Printed in China

First printing 2006

The restaurant industry thrives only because of the many hardworking permanent and part time employees who make up a given staff. Without this diverse group, we would all be cooking at home using cookbooks like this to enjoy a good meal.

-This book is dedicated to them.

Contents

Acknowledgments

During the past thirty years, my dad opened over a dozen restaurants as a management consultant and owner. He used the analogy that opening a new restaurant is a lot like attempting to produce and open a hit Broadway play. From the moment of inception, both require the concerted effort and synergy of many talented people, everyone working toward a common goal. It is the people mentioned here that made Va de Vi the successful restaurant it is today, and who made this book possible.

First and foremost we must acknowledge our Executive Chef, Kelly Degala, whose dedication and creative culinary skills has elevated Va de Vi to the forefront of the Bay Area restaurant scene. He is the star of this book.

Thanks to our inspirational Wine Director, Brendan Eliason, who with his superb knowledge of wine created an innovative and fun wine program that is unique to Va de Vi.

We thank our General Manager, Bob Cascardo, for his relentless passion for great food and wine, and for hiring and training our service staff. We are most appreciative to our entire staff for their dedication, especially those who have been with us from our opening.

We may never have finished this cookbook had it not been for our recipe consultant, Marlene Sorosky Gray, an accomplished cookbook writer in her own right. Marlene has taken Kelly's recipes to a place where we can all cook them at home. Her foreword reflects her passion for cooking.

We want to thank our landlord, Brian Hirahara of BH Development, for both his assistance during design and construction and for his ongoing support. Thanks to the city of Walnut Creek for their support and making the approval process relatively painless.

A typical day of problem solving during construction.

Our construction team was incredible. Architect Don Olsen and interior designer Catherine Macfee teamed to deliver a terrific floor plan and a fabulous décor. Contractor Ron Taylor and site foreman Gus Mee of Terra Nova Industries were invaluable in helping to resolve the myriad construction issues that occurred almost daily. They are true pros in the restaurant construction business. Thanks

also to Chuck Silverman for his lighting advice. For their artistic craftsmanship thanks go to Bill Empey, our glass designer, and to Russ Williams, our metal designer. For providing a beautiful product on a tight schedule, thanks go to glass artist Christina Spann for creating our distinctive sconces.

Chef Kelly Degala's reputation for outstanding presentation and food styling is evident in each photo in this cookbook. We thank photographers David Broach and Audrey Dempsey for capturing the very essence of each dish.

A special thanks to all of our mutual friends who diligently helped in testing Kelly's recipes: Leslie Kwartin, Nan Rust and Janet McClure.

This book started out as a collaborative effort of the partners of Va de Vi and their significant others. It was the proverbial problem of too many chefs in the kitchen and I ended up being the main writer. However, this book would not have been completed in a timely manner without the efforts of my wife Cindy, who provided help in all aspects of this book, from recipe testing to design layout and relentless editing. Her contribution was invaluable.

– Dale Raaen

Foreword
A Culinary Short Story

Chapter I. How It All Began

Once upon a time my husband and I were relaxing over lunch on Va de Vi's courtyard patio. Kelly was making the rounds and stopped at our table. We had met many months before in another restaurant setting and the conversation naturally turned to the day-to-day life of a chef. Kelly shared with me that plans were underway to write a cookbook. This was a new venture for Va de Vi's owners, as well as for Kelly. Having written several cookbooks, I couldn't help but wonder if they were aware that writing a cookbook is a far more complicated and arduous task than most readers realize. With that in mind, I wrote to Kelly suggesting that he might wish to take advantage of my expertise in authoring cookbooks.

Chapter II. Va de Vi Comes to My Kitchen

Getting started was, I think, more difficult than either of us expected. Kelly doesn't work from written recipes. He creates each dish almost intuitively. The challenge was to scale down his preparations for large-quantity recipes to recipes that could be made at home. Kelly and I cooked together in my kitchen twice a week for several months, making 3 to 4 recipes each time. He would tell me in advance what ingredients we needed and I would shop for them. That way I knew that the cookbook ingredients could be found at a supermarket or specialty food store.

While Kelly cooked, I followed him around from counter to oven to stovetop, furiously scribbling down the ingredients, their preparation and their presentation. There was a great reward at the end of the day when we sat down and sampled all the dishes. The food was always delicious and I never ceased to be amazed at how creative he was in combining different flavors and textures. And, the presentation was a work of art.

When Kelly left my real work began. I started by writing a first draft of each recipe. After several edits and often an initial test, the recipe was sent to the owners and a few friends. They then tested each recipe and we would critique the result in order to determine if it could be simplified, made ahead, or broken down and prepared in stages. In addition to getting the recipes on paper, Kelly was busy working with the owners on the very formidable task of self-publication. This included working with the photographers, designer and publisher. The result is a beautiful cookbook that features wonderful Va de Vi chef-quality recipes that can be cooked at home.

Chapter III. A Very Special Experience

Working with Kelly was a joy. He has an easy going manner, a terrific disposition and a great sense of humor. He is a pro who somehow always knows just what techniques and ingredients are needed to produce a superlative finished dish. In my career as a cooking teacher and cookbook author, I have worked with many great chefs: James Beard, Julia Child, Jacques Pepin and Wolfgang Puck among them. Kelly Degala's culinary knowledge, impeccable taste, creativity, and mastery of technique place him in the pantheon of the country's best chefs. When you try these recipes, you will be thrilled with the result, because Kelly's knowledge and taste shine through all of them.

Chapter IV. Va de Vi – A Destination Restaurant

The combination of ambience, service, energy and joie de vivre has been present from Va de Vi's inception and is the result of an initial collaborative effort that is ongoing. In large measure, the continued success of Va de Vi is due to Kelly's winning personality. I speak from experience that when Kelly stops by the table to chat, he leaves everyone smiling and glad to be dining with him. For those of us who enjoy eating out, a trip to Va de Vi is always rewarding.

– Marlene Sorosky Gray

Introduction

While under construction, passers-by paused to read the poster in the window announcing "Va de Vi Bistro and Wine Bar Opening Soon". Va—de—Vi they pronounced out loud. Then they said it again, smiling all the while. Va de Vi is fun to say.

Wine aficionados were filled with anticipation. Many became regulars before the doors even opened, stopping by to check on how construction was progressing. Business cards were left in the hopes of a grand opening invitation. Everyone, it seemed, from city officials to the ladies' lunch circuit to the hip crowd, was ready to welcome Va de Vi with open arms.

The idea to open Va de Vi began on a golf course in the spring of 2003 when my future partners, Stan Raaen and John Walz, and I discussed the possibility of opening an upscale wine bar and restaurant. It would be based on the model of a traditional European-style bistro, with an elegant but warm and friendly ambience. The restaurant would specialize in serving unique small plate dishes that would reflect an array of flavors from around the globe, complimented by a large selection of wines available by the glass.

Why this concept?

The food experience! *Due to the proliferation of foreign travel, the globalization of international cuisine has exploded in recent years, changing the way Americans eat. This change in the culinary world has been profound. Small plates dining is no longer a passing trend. It is a sensible as well as an exciting way to eat. Sharing one small plate feels like a snack, but by* sharing many, it becomes a meal. It's fun and casual and turns dining into a more convivial social experience. Small plates have existed in other cultures for centuries. Dim Sum, for instance, has delighted diners in China from the beginning of their cuisine. (Interestingly, dim sum means "touch the heart".) And then there's sushi. The Japanese believe that these small bites should satisfy all the senses. They are made with the freshest ingredients and are beautifully presented. In Turkish restaurants, small plates are called mezes, and Spanish tapas are perennial favorites.

The wine experience! While traveling or watching the food channel, Americans have developed an awareness of wine regions outside of California, whether it is Washington State, Chili or Australia. Va de Vi's wine philosophy is simple. Drink what you like with the food that you like. At Va de Vi, you have the opportunity to discover the wines you like best by sampling our wine flights. Wine flights are ideal for sharing, socializing and broadening your wine knowledge. Drinking wine is fun, and with the thousands of varietals and styles available it's a vast world to explore.

Bringing the Va de Vi concept to life was both fun and challenging. In the restaurant business the age-old adage applies. Location. Location. Location. After searching extensively, nothing seemed suitable. The possibilities were either off the beaten path, too big or too small. Then one day, we spotted a banner hanging across the front of a new building site. The banner read "Retail/Restaurant Space Available". The brick building with large windows and a very charming laneway adjacent to it was new, but it was designed to look old and historic. The laneway had space for outdoor seating with an added bonus – patio seating under a magnificent heritage oak tree. Moreover, the site was part of the renowned Walnut Creek outdoor mall district located on a main thoroughfare. To a restaurateur, the location rated a "10".

But, everyone agreed, the space was a bit small. Fitting in the obvious requirements of a kitchen, prep room and bathroom facilities, while still leaving room for sufficient dining space, would be a major challenge. Veteran architect Don Olsen rose to the challenge to solve our space problem. Interior designer Catherine Macfee joined the team to create the warm bistro atmosphere we envisioned. Creative juices flowed and drawing after drawing was reviewed and revised. Materials were agonized over. Voilà! At last, a winning design!

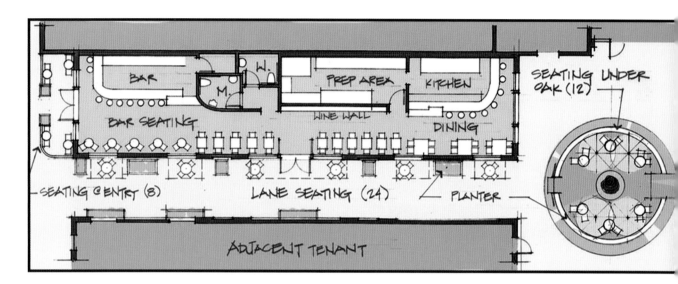

Va de Vi plans as drawn by architect Don Olsen.

Va de Vi evokes the feeling of an old Tuscan winery with a modern twist. A wine barrel effect was introduced by way of a curved ceiling and curved art wall in the center of the restaurant. Warm natural materials include French limestone, black tumbled marble, white Italian Carrera marble, aged walnut, custom-colored and hand-textured Italian plaster, hand-forged copper tiles with stainless steel inlay, custom copper surfaces, and hand-blown art glass wrapped in iron.

The place looked great, but one last detail remained. The small plates restaurant and wine bar needed a name. After extensive research on the Internet we discovered a name that we all loved, and couldn't have been more apropos to our concept – Va de Vi, which is Catalonian and loosely translates to "it's about wine." Perfect. Va de Vi Bistro and Wine Bar. It's about wine. It's about food. It's about having fun. It was about time to open and there were a few important details left to consider!

Our designer found inspiration in two five-foot tall French
shop in Napa. Originally used in the 1800's to crush grapes,
finish that has a rich patina from decades of use in the vineyards
wood stains and the rich color scheme

*Below: French wine press
corkscrews used in the 1800's
flank each side of the back bar.
Right: The walnut stained bar has
a copper top banded with custom
hand-pounded copper tiles inlaid
with stainless steel.*

*Right: Contemporary
elements include custom
hand-blown art glass
sconces with playful stripes
and hammered ironwork.*

antique wine press corkscrews that she discovered in an antique
these antique corkscrew columns have an aged mahogany
of France. The naturally-aged finish set the guideline for all the
throughout the restaurant.

Above: Flooring in the restaurant consists of both random planks of locally grown Napa walnut and French limestone and black tumbled marble. The natural elements and knots of the aged walnut were preserved to create the feeling of an old Tuscan winery. The basket weave pattern of the stone is reminiscent of a Paris bistro.

Finding a versatile chef skilled in global cuisine was our next challenge. After numerous interviews, it quickly became clear that Chef Kelly Degala was the perfect choice. Kelly's extensive background and experience enable him to marry the best techniques and flavors from around the world, cooking with the freshest locally-grown, raised or harvested ingredients. Each small plate Kelly serves is a savory, artistic creation.

Being a wine bar, Va de Vi needed a sommelier. However, the person we found for the job preferred the title "Head Wine Guy". The compromise was "Director of Wine". Brendan Eliason, a viticulture graduate of Cal-Poly and a winemaker in Sonoma, understands all aspects of wine and wine production and appreciates its diversity. He also believes wine should be fun, not stuffy. Restaurant veteran and wine enthusiast Bob Cascardo filled the key position of General Manager. His management experience and extensive knowledge of the local restaurant scene helped round out the leadership team.

As community excitement mounted, countless setbacks occurred in the attempt to open the restaurant as originally scheduled. The holiday season was the intended goal, but that goal

The Va de Vi management team enjoys a wine tasting. From left to right: Wine Director Brendan Eliason, owner John Walz, General Manager Bob Cascardo, Executive Chef Kelly Degala, and owners Dale and Stan Raaen.

disappeared before construction even began. January and February slipped away. Finally, on March 4, 2004, Va de Vi opened to the public. It was a grand evening.

What was clear from the beginning is that Va de Vi sparks conversation and conviviality. The lighting is flattering and soft. The dark wood and rich tones envelope diners in a comforting cocoon, yet the place is lively and full of energy. People are relaxed. They get to know their neighbors. *What's that you're having? Looks great.* Soon they find they have something in common (besides enjoying good food and wine) and are chatting away. Conversation, food and wine. What a delightful combination.

Why this cookbook? Va de Vi's success so far has been delivering great food, great wine and great service. While we can't deliver all these things to you, the reader, we can provide this cookbook and invite you to participate in our world of fine wine and cuisine at home. Traveling through the seasons, Chef Kelly Degala uses the freshest ingredients to take you on a culinary adventure of small plates with a global influence. Meanwhile, Wine Director Brendan Eliason is keeping pace in the vineyards, helping you discover wines from around the world to taste and enjoy.

At Va de Vi, exploration leads to discovery. Let the adventure begin!

The Va de Vi Wine Experience

The fun at Va de Vi starts when customers begin to read the tasting notes on our wine list written by our Wine Director, the mercurial Brendan Eliason. Brendan, co-winemaker at David Coffaro wines in Dry Creek, is known for his iconoclastic attitude toward wine (if drinking boxed wine from coffee cups is any indication). But no one disputes his knowledge of wine and ability to select good wines. Brendan's wine program at Va de Vi has received critical acclaim from many publications. Here are Brendan's thoughts on the Va de Vi wine program.

What Would Dionysus Do?

When the Greeks were choosing a god of wine, they did not choose the serious, logical Apollo; they did not choose Ares, the angry god of war; they chose Dionysus, a symbol of joy and merriment. The Greeks knew then what we sometimes forget now, that the principal purpose of wine is to improve our spirits and make our lives a little more fun.

The driving philosophy behind the wine program at Va de Vi is that no matter who you are, no matter what you like, we want you to leave our restaurant having enjoyed your food and wine experience, and like Dionysus, full of joy and merriment. Four things help us to encourage this experience and to differentiate the food and wine experience at Va de Vi: our selection of wines, our encouragement of customer experimentation, our wine-friendly food and our attempt to make wine tasting fun.

The challenge in putting together any wine list is that tasting and evaluating wine is highly subjective. There are as many different preferences as there are customers. Adding to this challenge are the millions of wines available in the world today, made from thousands of different grape varieties. If selecting from these wines were based on my personal preferences, the choices would be easy. The challenge is to narrow down the options to represent the broadest range of flavors, styles and regions possible.

Variety in style, country and price is the key. While we have many high-priced wines, we also carry many quality low-priced wines selected for their uniqueness and flavor. I am equally proud to carry Beringer white zinfandel and Caymus Special Select cabernet sauvignon on the list because each represents a style that a customer finds pleasurable.

Living in Northern California and working in the wine industry, it is easy to forget that drinking wine is still a relatively new experience for many people in this country. Wine as a cultural element is a recent development in the United States (beginning in the 1970s). When you consider that ninety percent of the wine consumed in this country is consumed by only ten percent of the population, you realize that America has more new than experienced wine drinkers. In this environment, encouraging experimentation is key to helping individuals discover wine styles and taste preferences.

How do you encourage experimentation? We attempt to do this by grouping taste portions into flights (at Va de Vi a wine flight is a set of 3-ounce pours of three different wines), having Mystery Flights and grouping wines by style on our bottle list.

Also, all of our wines by the glass include tasting

Pouring Wine:

1 ounce - adequate/small taste
2 ounces - average taste
3 ounces - generous taste
6 ounces - normal glass of wine
25.3 ounces - bottle

notes, meant to be informative, not overly scientific, but helpful as well as (hopefully) humorous. (See inset opposite page.)

The philosophy behind the flight system is the same philosophy behind the rest of the wine program, that everybody has different tastes and a good wine program should have something for everyone. All of Va de Vi's forty-eight wines by the glass are available in flights and in taste-sized pours. This flexibility gives people the opportunity to experiment and try new things.

Va de Vi's Jim Barry, not Australian wine producer Jim Barry.

Our wine tasting notes are intended to be both fun and informative, and they frequently invoke discussion among our patrons. The wine tasting note below serves as a good example.

2002 Jim Barry 'Lodge Hill', Shiraz, Clare Valley, Australia.

Who is the real Jim Barry? Is he a daring sea captain? Is he a dedicated farmer? Is he sitting on the stool next to you? Most sources seem to agree that he graduated college in 1947, but his record of larger-than-life exploits has caused many to wonder whether he really exists. This, of course, is ridiculous since whom else but Jim Barry could make this spicy, rich, minty dark cherry masterpiece? Drink, enjoy, and if you see Jim, tell him we said "Hi".

Jim Barry is a local Walnut Creek resident who frequents Va de Vi. Since Jim Barry also happens to be the name of a fine Australian winery, we decided to have some fun and add the wine to our wine list in honor of our Jim Barry. Little did we know how much fun we would have!

One night at the bar, a lady was reading the Jim Barry shiraz tasting notes aloud to a friend and exclaimed *right, like Jim Barry would be sitting next to us here.* As it happened, Jim was sitting next to them, and politely disclosed his presence. After much expression of disbelief, Jim displayed his drivers' license to prove he was in fact Jim Barry, leading to a good laugh for everyone at the bar.

If you don't know if you will like an Austrian gruner veltliner, you might not want to spend thirty dollars on a bottle. However, many people jump at the chance to try a taste for three dollars and seventy-five cents. They might be even more tempted to order a World White Flight and taste it next to a Spanish albarino and a pinot gris from Australia. If you know that you really love sauvignon blanc, order the Sauvignon Blanc Flight and compare and contrast examples of your favorite grape variety from Sonoma County, New Zealand and Bordeaux. Blind tasting, as done in our Mystery Flights, is another good way to learn and have fun exploring wine. We also encourage our customers to get creative and come up with their own flights. With twenty-four white wines and twenty-four red wines available in 3-ounce pours, there are over seventeen thousand combinations possible.

We have organized our white and red bottle list by style, according to the fruitiness, acidity, bitterness, spiciness and astringency that characterizes the wine. Within both the red and white lists, the wines styles go progressively from lighter to heavier styles.

White Wine Styles

Bubbles. When you think of how sparkling wine tastes, you think of the taste of classic French Champagne, dry and yeasty with hints of bread. For a change, try the other end of the spectrum where Italian prosecco is fresh, floral and fruity. In between the two is the typical style of sparkling wine produced in the United States, vibrant fresh fruit with elegance and depth.

Decadent - Sweet and Fruity. These wines all have some residual sugar, which leads to sweet fruit flavors. Wines in this style range from spicy gewürztraminer to floral muscat and sweet white zinfandel, but the classic in this category is riesling, especially German riesling. With a wide range of characteristics from light and acidic to rich, dense and honey luscious, there is a style to please everyone.

Aromatic - Floral and Rich. Viognier and dry riesling are the classic wines to stimulate your sense of smell; it's like being in a garden rich with floral and perfume scents. Some muscats, gewürztraminers and albarinos also fall in this category.

Snappy - Juicy and Brisk. Refreshing wines with lots of acidity, crispness, and citrus flavors make up this category. The headliner in this style is sauvignon blanc, but also included are pinot gris, verdelho, and many Italian and Spanish whites.

" Like drinking a citrus smoothie after a day at the spa. Mineral and floral notes with abundant citrus flavors and creaminess. Good and good for you, too"

2002 Valle Isarco, Pinot Grigio, Alto Adige, Italy

Bold – Smooth and Silky. Complex and fruit driven, these wines reflect the basic character of the grape variety. Tastes of apples, pears and peaches are the driving characters, along with the occasional hints of mineral. Gruner vetliner, French chardonnay and roussanne can all be of this style, as can some pinot gris.

Voluptuous – Full and Oaky. The flavors in this style reflect the intervention of winemakers. Most are heavily treated with oak. They are also made using various levels of malolactic fermentation that makes the wine creamy and rich with loads of vanilla and hints of butterscotch.

In between white and red is the Pink Pride Dry Rosé style. Crisp and acidic, these wines are soft, juicy reds with flavors of roses, fresh cherries and strawberries. Typically these are made from Rhone grape varieties such as grenache and syrah.

In summer in the south of France, French rosé classics like Domaine Tempier or Tavel can be found at nearly every bistro table.

Red Wine Styles

Mild – Soft and Fruity. These wines have few mouth-drying tannins, and thus are very smooth. Grenache and cabernet franc are good examples, but gamay-based wines from the Beaujolais region in France best exemplify this style.

Mild – Full and Smooth. When people order "a glass of red wine", this is the style they are expecting. The wines are extremely well balanced in acid, fruit extraction and tannins. Merlot, pinot noir and malbec are often made in this style.

Yummy – Jammy and Spicy. Using moderate to heavily ripened grapes, these assertive wines invoke the flavors of various jams, often with nutmeg, cinnamon or pepper. Zinfandel, French Rhone wines or shiraz from warm-climate Australia are found in this style.

Burly – Dense and Intense. These wines are fruit bombs exploding with flavor -- big, bold and dark from the heavy fruit extraction. Highly tannic with lots of oak, this style typifies the New World wines of California, Argentina and Australia. Cabernet sauvignon and blends dominate this category, but it also includes many other grape varieties such as barbera and tempranillo.

" This wine is like mud wrestling with the Dallas Cowboy cheerleaders; yeah, it's kind of earthy, but it's so soft and full-bodied that you're not likely to complain. "

2000 Lincourt Cellars, Syrah, Santa Barbara County

So if you have a favorite wine, you can experiment with other varieties that match its style.

The experience we are trying to create comes together at the table with the melding of food, wine and friends. With many interesting dishes and a wide selection of wine, a common question from guests is what wine goes with what dish. When they find out that we avoid food and wine pairing, people are intrigued and sometimes confused. The premise behind putting specific wines with specific foods ignores individual differences and preferences; it is also difficult in an environment where sharing multiple small plates is the norm. Instead, we present customers with a range of fascinating flavors and a wine program that encourages experimentation. This lets them sample and

choose the wine they like with the food they like.

Is there an impact on wine taste when pairing food and wines? The answer is yes. There are some basic reactions between food and wine; whether these are good or bad depends on personal preference. For example, salt flavors and acid flavors in food tend to make wine taste milder (experience this by drinking cabernet sauvignon shots with salt and lime, really, it's fascinating). Alternately, sweet and protein flavors tend to make wines taste stronger. Is that good? Is that bad? The answer is a definite maybe, sometimes, depending on what you like. Some people like mild, some people like strong. Everybody's tastes are different (see related article *A Matter of Taste* – page 18).

Food and wine reactions are complex and dependent on all the ingredients in a recipe. People often talk about the right wine pairing for steak or seafood without thinking about the seasonings and sauces served with them, which can have a huge impact on the reaction with wine. Look at the cuisine of countries with strong wine traditions and you will see how they have used seasonings to balance their meals and often neutralize the reaction with wine. Steak is high in protein, which can make wines taste stronger. Adding salt (making the wine taste milder) balances the steak and enables you to drink whatever you want. In countries such as France, Spain and Italy, people developed, through trial and error, cuisines that were balanced and therefore went well with local wines, red or white.

Try this experiment with several people, each with their favorite wine. Cook a steak, but don't add any seasoning, and then taste it with whatever wine you are drinking. Next, add a few shakes of salt and a squeeze of lime to the steak and taste it again. The balanced dish (meat, salt, lime juice) should taste better with each of the different wines. You might be amazed (or hopefully at least amused), but this fact comes as no surprise to Italians; they have long enjoyed eating this traditional Tuscan dish, Bistecca alla Fiorentina, with their favorite red or white wines.

Kelly Degala's recipes in this cookbook are all wonderfully balanced and will pair well with all styles of wine. For example, the Pan-Fried Crab Cakes, which are high in protein, are balanced with the garlic, red pepper and Dijon mustard in the recipe. In addition, the garnishes Kelly uses with his recipes not only make the presentation beautiful but also help balance the food, a la the pickled cucumber with the crab cakes or the kimchee with the Kalbi Flat Iron Steak. The balanced food in this book should make your food and wine experience a pleasure.

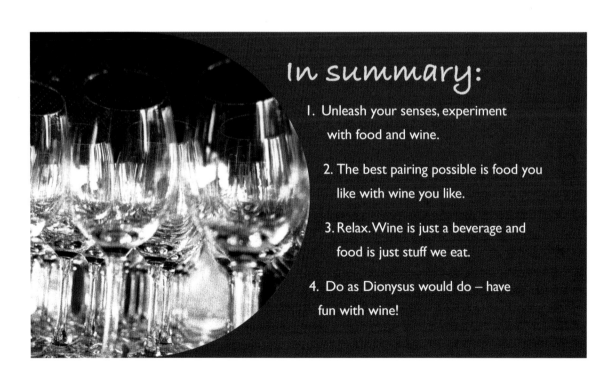

In summary:

1. Unleash your senses, experiment with food and wine.

2. The best pairing possible is food you like with wine you like.

3. Relax. Wine is just a beverage and food is just stuff we eat.

4. Do as Dionysus would do – have fun with wine!

A Matter of Taste

Food and wine lie at the intersection of sustenance and joy. Nutritionally, we can live by consuming the most basic of nutritional components: so many proteins, fats and carbohydrates, so many vitamins and minerals. Instead, the act of eating and drinking has become an integral part of our cultural and social interactions. We did not evolve the ability to taste and smell so we could enjoy a Meyer-lemon infused crème brûlée; we developed these senses so we would not die from poisoning, disease or starvation. Our senses of taste and smell have remained unchanged for millions of years, yet we have only recently begun to understand how taste senses work.

Taste

We have the ability to perceive five tastes: sweet, sour (acidic), bitter, salt and umami. Unless you make a habit of reading current research in sensory science journals, the last taste, umami, may not be familiar to you. Umami is the taste of protein (or glutamate to be more specific) and has only been proven definitively in the last decade. Umami is the primary taste in food such as ripe tomatoes, broth, Parmesan cheese and a mother's milk. Along with sweet, umami tells your body that the food you have in your mouth is safe and nutritious.

Bitterness and acidity serve a complimentary role in food safety. In nature, poisons are often bitter and foods that have spoiled are often acidic. Therefore, we are naturally leery of foods with these qualities.

Salt is desired because our bodies cannot store it and it is vital for many of our basic life functions. Since the average Westerner consumes ten times more salt than is needed (one to three grams per day would suffice), salt is a case where social usage has driven consumption past the point of need. Today, salt is primarily used as a food preservative and bitterness suppressant/flavor enhancer.

Snowflakes

One interesting aspect of taste is the range of diversity among individuals, so much so that no two people share the same sensitivity to tastes. Sometimes the differences are small; sometimes they are large. The two primary aspects of taste are encompassed by its dictionary definition:

1. The sense that distinguishes the sweet, sour, salty, protein and bitter qualities of dissolved substances in contact with the taste buds on the tongue.

2. A personal preference or liking.

These definitions highlight the influences of nature and nurture on individual taste and acknowledge that tastes are unique to individuals.

One example of differences in taste is the existence of the so-called super tasters. Scientists have been able to isolate the ability to taste certain bitter compounds down to a single gene. Depending on whether the two alleles of this gene are dominant and/or recessive, twenty-five percent of the world has a low number of taste buds and a high threshold to bitterness, fifty percent are average and the last twenty-five percent have a high number of taste buds and are extra sensitive to bitterness. This also correlates to sensitivity for sweetness, spiciness and other flavors. Thus, no matter who you are, at least half of the world has significantly different genetic taste sensitivity than you.

There are other factors that make taste an individual matter. Preferences change over time. For example, hormone changes in women alter their taste sensitivity and peoples' tastes tend to dull as they get older. Social factors also play a role. With enough will power we can acquire a taste for a wide range of foods and beverages that our genetics may think are poison. This is how we learn to enjoy bitter or acidic substances like coffee and Scotch whiskey (and dry red wine). Experiences in life can also have an influence. If your mother used to make you chicken soup when you were sick, you may have an affinity for that soup now because it makes you feel comforted. However, if you were raised on a chicken farm, the taste of chicken soup might not be so comforting.

In the end, surprise, surprise, we're all different. Drink accordingly.

- Brendan Eliason

Recreating the Va de Vi

Wine flights are an integral part of the experience at Va de Vi. Luckily, recreating this wine experience is something you can do in the comfort of your own home. The general principle is more wine equals more fun. The specifics are slightly more complicated, but anyone with an advanced viticulture degree and access to a commercial wine laboratory will find the process only moderately difficult. Alternatively, you can just finish reading this section.

So how does the average person recreate the Va de Vi experience at home? First the bad news, it doesn't work well with only one or two people. You'll need to throw a party. Now the good news, you can get other people to bring the wine. All you need is a plan.

1

Step one is to pick a wine tasting theme. Possibilities include:

- **An assortment of wines made from the same grape variety,** e.g., zinfandel, syrah, sauvignon blanc, etc. This is a great way to compare and contrast different styles from different regions, or different winemakers from the same region. One example is the Sauvignon Blanc Flight previously mentioned. Sauvignon blanc from New Zealand is typically very grassy and has lots of tropical flavors, while California fume blanc is typically made with oak and has toasty flavors. Another example is a shiraz/syrah tasting. Australia is a big country and shiraz styles from different regions are dramatically different. Cool climate Victoria is typically leaner and more peppery than hot climate Barossa shiraz, which is usually rich, lush and heavy with flavors of oak. These wines are also very different from Syrah produced in California or France. In the end, you will discover which region or style you like best for a particular variety.

Wine Experience at Home

- **Wines from the same country/region** e.g., South America, Italy, Bordeaux, etc. As an example, you can explore the mystery of French wines. What exactly is Bordeaux wine, and are wines from Pomeral different from Pauillac? Is Cote du Rhone different than Cote du Rhone-Villages? And why doesn't the label tell you what the grapes are in the wine? With a little research and a few parties, you can begin to make a dent into the mysteries of French wine. You can do the same for Germany, Spain and others.

- **Wines that fit a general taste category** or style, e.g., oak and buttery, crisp and acidic, soft or fruity, intense and tannic, etc. Which chardonnay style do you like best? Is your preference a lot of oak and butter, or the mineral style typically found in French chardonnays? Likewise, do you like reds that make you pucker from the tannins, are soft and fruity, or are fruit bombs of intense flavor?

- **Rare or unusual wines.** Ever hear of zweigelt? Pelorsin? Charbonno? These are just a few of the over two thousand wine varietals being produced in the world today. One party; 6 wine varietals; only 1,994 wine varietals to go.

- **Blind tasting.** An interesting variation on any theme is to train to recognize wines by blind tasting. First, taste each wine and make notes describing what you see, smell, and taste. Then, taste each wine blind to see if you can pick which wine is which. Hah, the New Zealand sauvignon blanc's grassy nose gives it away every time.

- **Whatever stirs your creative juices.** Since the point is to experiment and have fun, just about any theme can work: female winemakers, unique blends, wines costing less than five dollars (slip a thirty dollar bottle into the mix and see what happens), or wines made with crazy names or labels.

You can always get ideas from the Va de Vi flights. For our current selection of flights, check us out at va-de-vi-bistro.com

2

Step two of the plan is to pick several different wines that fit the chosen theme.

Based on ample scientific research (if parties at my place qualify), I've found that five to six different wines work quite well for a party. More than six wines starts to get confusing (especially once you start drinking, which is the point).

3

Step three is deciding how many people you want to have over (and therefore how much wine you'll need).

One bottle is enough for ten people to get an average taste with a small margin of error (assuming 2-ounce tastes). Since you are choosing six different wines for tasting, this means that for every ten people you need one bottle of each different wine. Twenty people means two bottles of each different wine, etc.

This calculation is based upon each person drinking two glasses of wine (12 ounces) in total plus a margin of error. (It is always better to have extra wine at the end of a party instead of no wine). This number can easily be adjusted up or down based on your group. Some people look at two glasses of wine and think *Two? In the same night?* Others look at two glasses of wine and think *Yeah, that's enough to sip on while I decide what I really want to drink.* Plan accordingly.

As Stephen Stills said *if you can't be with the one you love, love the one you're with*, so if you can't make it to Va de Vi, recreate the experience wherever you are. Cheers.

– Brendan Eliason

The Va de Vi Food Experience

Creative and unique are two words that describe our Executive Chef Kelly Degala and his global small plates menu. The bold, balanced flavors that typify Kelly's culinary style are showcased in each small plate served at Va de Vi. In addition to Kelly's expertise in the kitchen, his can-do attitude and attention to detail energize the entire restaurant. Here's Kelly's account of his diverse background and experience.

I feel very fortunate to have become a chef. I don't think you choose to be a chef; it's something that chooses you. My first job in the restaurant business was working as a valet parking cars and as a bus boy; then I started working in the kitchen as a pantry cook. I was told I was good at it, and when you're told you are good at something at a very young age, you say, **Okay, maybe I should keep on doing this**. Twenty-eight years later, it is still very satisfying to have my food be well received and to have regular customers who appreciate what I do. I just want to keep on being a chef and continue experimenting and creating exceptional cuisine.

There have been many chefs who have influenced me through the years, but my mom influenced me the most. My parents immigrated to Hawaii from the Philippines. Their village was right off the beach, so one of their staples was seafood. That was my mom's forte and, without a doubt, one of the reasons I like to feature fresh seafood on my menus. My mom would cook wonderful Filipino dishes such as lumpia, pancit, adobo, and sinigang; I could go on and on. Being new to America, she also wanted to cook traditional American dishes such as steak, eggs, pot roast and ribs. American cooking in Hawaii was extremely diverse, being influenced by Japanese, Chinese, Portuguese and Italian immigrants. I didn't just grow up with Filipino cuisine and American cuisine; I grew up with an array of cuisines that have become part of my flavor profile, the different combinations of flavors I like to use when cooking.

Tom Douglas was the chef who taught me how to work with the flavor profiles I had collected and had a great influence on my style of cooking. I had just moved to Seattle in 1984. Tom hired me as his morning line cook for two reasons: I could cook eggs and I could make beurre blanc. The restaurant was called Café Sport and before I knew it I was reading great reviews and articles about Tom and the restaurant. I was pretty impressed by all the media attention he was getting, but what impressed me more was the ingredients he brought into the restaurant, like goat cheese from Sally Jackson and wild mushrooms from Peter Gordon. Here was a chef from the East Coast using local West Coast ingredients along with Asian ingredients such as seaweed salad, Chinese sauces and pickled ginger. How did he make it all work? Tom told me he liked to try all kinds of food; he loved to eat. When he tasted something he liked, he would try to recreate it, not a bastardized version, but a Tom Douglas version. It didn't have to be an authentic recreation as long as it had the flavor dynamics he wanted. Tom helped me put things together. I started thinking about all the cuisines I had been exposed to and how I could create my own recipes.

Two other Seattle chefs who were influential in my style of cooking are Caprial Pence and Jim Han Lock. I worked with Caprial at a restaurant called Fullers. She was only 24 years old and the executive chef at probably *the* premier restaurant in Seattle. Caprial had a natural ability to create dishes very quickly, yet very elegantly. She knew how to pair flavors together. Like Tom, she enjoyed Asian influences. Caprial and I would often discuss different Asian ingredients and how they could work in different dishes. I was impressed by her ability to make cooking look so simple and yet have it be so creative. The more I watched her cook, and cooked with her, the more I learned.

I worked with Jim Han Lock at Wild Ginger, an upscale Asian restaurant. Jim took Asian cooking to a different level. It wasn't just simple Asian cuisine, it was amazing, diverse Asian cuisine blending flavors and ingredients from different regions – China, Korea, Thailand, Viet Nam, you name it. Even though the restaurant was high volume, Jim still presented plates in a beautiful way, very similar to the way we present our small plates at Va de Vi.

One common factor in working with all three chefs is that I learned a lot about using fresh, regional ingredients. Each restaurant was different from the other, but all utilized local ingredients. Just like the Pacific Northwest, Northern California has much to offer in the way of fresh, quality local ingredients. All three chefs are James Beard Award winners; I was very lucky to have the opportunity to work with each of them.

Another person that I would have to say impacted me would be my wife, Kirsti, who encouraged me to explore Mediterranean and Italian cuisines. Kirsti helped me to further broaden my flavor profiles and cooking skills so that today I have a wide range of knowledge to draw upon.

So, after growing up and watching my mom cook, working with three great chefs, gathering all these flavor profiles and cooking techniques, you know what? I said to myself, *Hey, I can do this!* That is when the experimentation began. The positive results didn't happen overnight, but they did happen eventually. I began to feel more and more comfortable meshing flavors, meshing techniques, Asian and non-Asian, and putting it all together to produce good food.

The best thing about being chef at Va de Vi is the freedom I've been given to use everything I've learned the last twenty-eight years. I like to cook with big flavors, a wide variety of flavors from all over the world. When all these flavors come rushing at you, how do you react? That's what it's all about at Va de Vi.

I grew up eating a variety of foods from different parts of the world, which is why I feel so at ease with the global cuisine at Va de Vi. Let's put it

this way, when you come to Va de Vi you're visiting a lot of countries all in one place. Our guests can order a Spanish inspired paella, Asian inspired ahi tartare (my version is influenced by the Hawaiian dish Poke), a French-based Niçoise salad, Filipino pork ribs adobo, and a California/Italian inspired porcini risotto all in one sitting.

Ahi Tempura Roll

Incorporating all these different cuisines and ingredients into a small plates menu is challenging, but a lot of fun. There are currently twenty-eight items on our menu, offering a wide selection of vegetable, fish, and meat dishes with a variety of flavor profiles. We change the menu often to coincide with the availability of the freshest, seasonal ingredients. This, combined with the specials we offer, keeps our menu fresh for the guests who come to the restaurant frequently. They can further enhance their experience by experimenting with different wines from around the world to go with their food. It's all very creative, from putting together a diverse menu to the choices of food and wine made by our guests.

Va de Vi means it's about wine in Catalan, but, to my way of thinking, wine and food is what it's about! Enjoy! Bon appétit! Or in Catalan, bon profit!

– Kelly Degala

Having a Small Plates Party at Home

Planning a small plates dinner party at home requires time and a lot of ingredients. It is much easier to do small plates at home if you have several people contributing – the more chefs the better.

If you're doing small plates for only two, choose three recipes and have fun. On the other hand, let's say you decide to have eight dinner party guests. Assuming you are sharing plates like we do at Va de Vi, plan on five recipes to have enough food for

Spring

Summer

Spring
- Asparagus Salad with Manchego Cheese and Serrano Ham
- Grilled Pork Satay with Spicy Peanut Sauce
- Seared Alaskan Halibut with Thai Red Curry Sauce
- Sautéed Savoy Spinach with Lemon, Garlic and Tomatoes
- Grilled Rib-Eye Steak with Fingerling Potatoes, Cipollini Onions and Roquefort Sauce

Summer
- Basil Marinated Mozzarella with Heirloom Tomatoes
- Hoisin-Glazed Baby Back Pork Ribs
- Grilled Alaskan Wild Ivory King Salmon with Yukon Gold Mashed Potatoes and Creamed Corn
- Grilled Tiger Prawn Satay with Thai Red Curry Sauce
- Grilled Parma Prosciutto-Wrapped Ambrosia Melon and Beefsteak Tomato Sorbet

everyone to be satisfied. Menu suggestions for each season have a mix of recipes, some of which can be made a day or two ahead or at least partially ahead. For preparation advice, check out the Countdown box contained in most of our recipes.

Up to 2 weeks ahead	Up to 2 days ahead	1 day ahead	Up to 4 hours ahead
Spicy Peanut Sauce Thai Red Curry Sauce Pickled Cucumbers	Strawberry Papaya-Mint Relish Spanish Sherry Vinaigrette Roquefort Sauce	Marinate pork Marinate steak	Cook asparagus Green Papaya Salad

This chart is a sample of how to organize the preparation time for your small plates party at home based on the spring menu listed below.

Fall

Winter

Fall

- Hoisin-Glazed Lamb Chops with Wasabi Mashed Potatoes
- Crab Cakes with Avocado, Aioli and Citrus Butter Sauce
- Lacquered Quail with Garlic Fried Rice and Fried Spinach
- Seared Hawaiian Big Eye Tuna with Sake-Wasabi Butter Sauce on Potato Croquette
- Grilled Radicchio and Porcini Mushroom Salad with Smoked Idiazabal and Fig Balsamic Vinaigrette

Winter

- Rock Shrimp and Avocado Lumpia with Wasabi-Orange Cream
- Endive and Frisée Salad with Gala Apples, Marcona Almonds and Roquefort
- Rioja Braised Beef Short Ribs with Creamy Polenta
- Meatballs and Orchiette in Tomato Sauce
- Yellow and Red Beet Salad with Arugula, Goat Cheese and Fried Shallots

An Interview with Chef Kelly Degala

What is your favorite cuisine?

I enjoy all cuisines, but Asian and Italian intrigue me the most. Asian cuisine is my forte and I enjoy using Asian ingredients in non-Asian dishes. If I were to re-invent myself as a chef, it would be to cook Italian cuisine.

How would you define small plates?

Some people confuse small plates with tapas. I define them by how many bites it takes to finish the dish. Tapas take two to three bites. A small plate requires about five bites. Anything beyond that, maybe past seven bites, would be an entrée to me. A small plate doesn't have to consist of just one item; it can be a steak, a starch and a vegetable presented in a manner where you still have just five to seven bites, nothing more.

How important are the quality of the ingredients when you cook?

Very important. Even something as simple as salt is important. When I use salt it's usually a sea salt, so most of the recipes in this book call for sea salt. In Hawaii I started using alaea, which is a red sea salt. When I was in Washington State I added fleur de sel, a French sea salt to the ingredients I use. In California I have added another salt, grey salt, which I use mostly for finishing.

What do you mean by finishing?

Finishing is the final step in completing a dish. As part of the presentation, garnishes I use include: fried shallots, fried herbs, sturgeon caviar, organic herbs, house made crème fraîche or ponzu sauce, truffles and Japanese pickled vegetables. I do it to highlight the ingredient itself, not to overwhelm the dish.

I stock a wide variety of quality olive oils in our restaurant, many of which I use for finishing. I use lemon oil on our crab cakes, blood-orange oil on our grilled asparagus. A good extra virgin olive oil finishes our pastas, whereas I use porcini

Tuna Sashimi Rosette finished with togarashi, furikake, tobiko and blood orange oil.

oil on our risotto. I use black and white truffle oil on different types of fishes and on mashed potatoes.

Quality balsamic vinegar is also very important. I use eighteen-year-old balsamic vinegar for finishing a grilled rib-eye steak, among other items. Of course, my favorite is thirty-year-old balsamic vinegar. It's expensive so I use it lightly to finish, for example, strawberries, beef tenderloin and grilled porcinis or chanterelles. When I taste great thirty-year-old balsamic vinegar by itself, I can identify its amazing qualities right away. My mind starts imagining all of the wonderful possibilities I can combine it with.

This is why I enjoy cooking at Va de Vi. I have quality ingredients that I can mix and match and come up with great combinations. It's like pairing wine and food. You don't necessarily have just one wine that goes with one dish; wine is easily paired with other dishes that you never thought of pairing it with and often, surprisingly, it works. At Va de Vi the boundaries are removed, allowing me to experiment with a wide variety of ingredients and products.

How important is your relationship with local farmers and vendors?

I have the highest, the utmost respect, for local farmers. They are true artisans; they make a product from the ground up, literally, and not only do they grow it, they harvest it, sell it, and in most cases they also deliver it. The quality is different when you get produce from specialty farmers than when you get commercial produce that is mass-produced. One of my vendors is Knoll Farms, which is located in Brentwood, California. Their torpedo onion not only looks beautiful, it tastes beautiful. We do business with other farmers out of Brentwood, such as Brookside Farms, where we get fava beans, plums and pluots, which is a combination of plum and apricot. It's products like these that make you want to do business with specialty farmers.

We have another very interesting local vendor, King of Mushrooms. You can't miss Todd Spanier the king, when he walks through your door because he's over seven feet tall. His love for mushrooms has led him to become one of the top sellers in Northern California. I get truffles from him in addition to porcinis, morels and piopinis. Talking to Todd, you learn a lot about the different types of mushrooms and when they are in season. Tom also supplies me with different oils, such as porcini and black truffle oil. He also brings other exotic products such as wild asparagus from France and Poheli Farms ferns from the Big Island of Hawaii.

Ahi Brothers is another important vendor. They supply us with Dungeness crab meat and Hokkaido scallops, the ingredients in two of our most popular dishes. However, the main item they supply us with is sushi-grade tuna. Their tuna has been of exceptional quality since the first day I ordered from them. Ken Enomoto is not just a businessman; he loves the products he sells. He doesn't look for the least expensive product; he looks for the best price for the best product. I am impressed with that.

One of my favorite vendors right now is Giuseppe Cagnoni from Etruria, an Italian gourmet food importer. We use his white and black truffles and olive oils. His product is just phenomenal. When you taste a teaspoon of his olive oil from Italy, you say, *Hey, I'm going to have another teaspoon.* Suddenly you find yourself sipping olive oil. Not many people sip olive oil, but once you taste his olive oil you'll understand.

He also supplies us with bottarga di muggine, the dried roe sac of grey mullet that we use in our risotto, and grains like farro and lentils.

In addition to the main produce companies I use throughout the year, in the summer I do business with as many as six or seven more. Each company has a specialty item that I can't wait to incorporate into my menu. It may sound crazy, and it is difficult to manage sometimes, but the purpose in working with so many vendors, farmers, and specialty providers is to secure the best products available.

First year of opening:

3,298 pounds of tuna

2,555 pounds of crab cakes

25,331 flights of wine

5,868 by the bottle sales

172,760 wine glasses washed

105,000 dinner guests

252,917 plates of food

Q What kitchen equipment do people need that they probably don't have?

Sharp knives. Nine out of ten times, when I go to someone's house to cook, they'll have a knife that is so dull that it shouldn't even be used. I

enjoy using my knives. If my knives are not sharp, chances are I'm not going to feel like cooking. My advice is to buy good knives and have them sharpened, once a year, at your local grocery or sharpening outlet.

One of the most important items in my kitchen is my Japanese mandolin. I also use my Kitchen Aide with a whisk and the attachment dough hook for baking. I like whisks of all sorts, sizes and shapes. If I have ten whisks in front of me when making dinner, I'll probably use all ten.

One piece of equipment I particularly love, especially in summer, is my grill. Everyone needs an outdoor grill.

I use charcoal or wood; I prefer having a natural fire rather than gas. I use a lot of wood chips to add a smoky scent to whatever I'm cooking.

Your food drawings are very interesting. When did you start drawing food, and why?

My wife, Kirsti, says that I've been doing it since she's known me. We've been married fifteen years, but I actually don't remember exactly when I started drawing. I guess it started when I was in college. I was debating between becoming an architect or an electrical engineer.

I guess we know where that went. Anyway, I took a lot of courses that required drawings and that's how I developed my drawing style. I don't consider myself an artist, per se.

I like to draw the dishes I am creating in order to give the staff, both the kitchen and the front of the house, a visualization of what I'm going to present. I envision the dish in my mind – the ingredients, the colors. I sit down with colored pencils or crayons and draw a general sketch. Then, I

Kelly's cookbook collection.

break it down by ingredients, sauces, etc., It's not perfect, but I think it helps the staff get an idea of what the finished dish is going to look like.

I especially like to make drawings when we have special events. This past New Year's Eve, Va de Vi had an eight-course prix fix menu that featured dishes totally different and a bit more complicated than our everyday menu. To prepare the staff for this special evening, I created a small portfolio of drawings of every dish. I think the sketches not only helped the staff appreciate the food, they also made them feel involved in the process.

Do you have a cookbook fetish?

(Laughter) A cookbook is more than a cookbook to me. I've always dreamed about traveling, but so far I haven't been able to travel as much as I'd like. So, for me, a cookbook is a way to travel, helping me to imagine being in that country or region. When I buy and read an Italian cookbook, I can imagine myself being in Tuscany, looking at the harvest, watching the farmers at work, and seeing the fisherman bringing home their bounty. Cookbooks offer great adventures and stories.

Usually I buy a cookbook to learn more about a particular cuisine. In the early part of my career, I bought Asian cookbooks. I probably have every good cookbook on Thai, Vietnamese, Japanese, Chinese and Korean cooking ever written. I read them and I look at the pages over and over again until I understand the philosophical aspects of the cuisine. The photos are important, too; they help visualize the dish. I collect cookbooks because of the imagination and creativity they invoke.

There are a lot of cookbooks that inspire me. Thomas Keller's *French Laundry Cookbook* is phenomenal. It's not easy, and it's definitely aimed at a professional chef or a serious home cook, but you can feel his passion. If I don't feel passion for cooking in a cookbook, chances are I won't like it. Another inspirational cookbook is from Tetsuya Wakuda, a Japanese-born chef who is considered the best chef in Australia. When you look at his food, it's beautiful and it tastes amazing. One thing I say when I teach food presentation is, *if it looks beautiful then it's going to taste beautiful.*

Cookbooks are my way of keeping up with who's doing what and understanding how other chefs use certain ingredients. There is a cookbook from Mario Batali, titled *The Babbo Cookbook*, which always gives me the urge to cook Italian food. When you read what he creates, you want to start cooking and eating.

I love reading stories about chefs; where they've been, whom they've worked for, what they are doing now and what they want to do next. When a chef has more than one cookbook, and when you read their second or third book, you realize that they're still doing what they love to do. This has led to a collection of literally hundreds of cookbooks that have devoured almost two walls in my home. It's a bit out of control because we're running out of room in the office. (Chuckle).

Q **What is your favorite food?**

That's easy. Ahi tartare. I could eat ahi tartare for breakfast, lunch and dinner. And if I need a midnight snack, the first thing that comes to mind is ahi tartare.

Spring

For winemakers, the symbolic beginning of spring in the vineyard is always the same. As winter fades away and the days get warmer, each of the thirty to forty buds on every vine starts slowly swelling larger and larger until, pop, it bursts forth, covering the dark, woody vines with pea-sized green popcorn kernels. This bursting forth is called bud break and it is the first tangible sign of the year to come.

These buds rapidly develop into long, slender green shoots that stretch towards the sky and spread their new leaves, like wings, to catch the life-giving rays of the sun. As the shoots grow, miniature clusters continually unfold themselves from the base of each shoot, slowly expanding from less than one half inch long to the size of a pack of cards. The skinny stalks of the immature clusters are haphazardly dotted with tiny clusters of buds, each of which will turn into grapes if fertilized when the vine blooms. Once fertilized, the cluster grows longer and wider until it starts to resemble normal looking grapes.

To match the aromas of fresh spring food, try some wines with the style **Aromatic –Floral and Rich**. Try a viognier or a Spanish albarino; both typically have a very floral nose. For red wines, try a cabernet franc, which can smell like violets and fresh cut peppers.

-Brendan Eliason

Spring is the beginning of what food is all about; it's like an explosion. Spring brings morels, porcinis and asparagus. March is the beginning of the halibut season; black cod becomes available out of Alaska. Spring gives me the opportunity to present ingredients in their pure form.

-Kelly Degala

Spring Recipes

Grilled Rib-Eye Steak
with fingerling potatoes, cipollini onions and roquefort sauce

When you taste tangy, salty Roquefort together with sweet, acidic balsamic vinegar you'll wonder why you haven't paired the two flavors sooner. The combination of tender strips of grilled organic, grass fed steak coated with a ribbon of creamy Roquefort cheese and drizzled with balsamic vinegar is a match made in heaven.

TIPS:

- Ask the butcher to trim the rib-eye steak, leaving the center cut which has less fat. If desired, save the trimmings for stew.
- The only time-consuming step in making the marinade is removing the thyme stems from the leaves. If you include the thin, tender stems with the leaves (not the heavy wooden ones) it will save time.

COUNTDOWN

Up to 2 days ahead
- Make Roquefort sauce.
- Make marinade.

1 day ahead
- Marinate steaks and refrigerate.

4 hours ahead
- Marinate steaks at room temperature.
- Bring Roquefort sauce to room temperature.

1 hour ahead
- Prepare coals.
- Roast potatoes and onions.

20 minutes before serving
- Grill potatoes, onions and steaks.

INGREDIENTS

ROQUEFORT SAUCE
3 ounces Roquefort cheese (½ cup)
3 tablespoons buttermilk

GARLIC AND THYME MARINADE
1 cup extra virgin olive oil
1 shallot, peeled and quartered
6 cloves garlic, peeled
½ cup thyme leaves (¾ ounce on stems)
1 tablespoon black peppercorns
1 cup Italian parsley leaves
1 dried or fresh bay leaf

STEAKS, POTATOES AND ONIONS
1 pound beef rib-eye, center cut trimmed, cut into ¾- to 1-inch thick steaks (4 ounces each)
8 fingerling potatoes with peel, scrubbed
4 cipollini onions, peeled
2 teaspoons extra virgin olive oil
1 teaspoon sea salt

PRESENTATION
Balsamic vinegar
Extra virgin olive oil
4 sprigs Italian parsley

TO MAKE ROQUEFORT SAUCE: In a small bowl, stir cheese to soften it. Stir in buttermilk. Use immediately or refrigerate for up to 2 days. Use at room temperature.

TO MAKE MARINADE: In a blender, blend all ingredients until pureed. Use immediately or refrigerate up to 2 days. Makes 1 cup.

TO MARINATE STEAKS: Put steaks into a plastic zipper bag. Pour marinade over and toss to coat. Refrigerate overnight, turning occasionally. Marinate at room temperature for 4 hours before grilling.

TO ROAST POTATOES AND ONIONS: Preheat oven to 400°F. Put potatoes and onions into a shallow baking pan. Drizzle with 2 teaspoons olive oil; toss to coat. Sprinkle with 1 teaspoon sea salt. Cover with foil. Bake for 10 to 15 minutes. Timing will depend on size of onions; they should have a little give when centers are pierced with a skewer. Remove onions to a plate. Cover potatoes and bake 20 more minutes or until almost tender. Remove foil and continue to bake uncovered for 10 to 15 minutes or until tender. Cool potatoes; cut in half lengthwise. Cut onions in half.

TO GRILL STEAKS, POTATOES AND ONIONS: Oil grill grate and prepare coals or preheat gas grill to high. Grill potatoes and onions cut side down until grill marks appear and they are heated through. Move to cooler part of grill to keep warm. Remove steaks from marinade (do not wipe excess marinade from meat) and season with sea salt and pepper. Grill steaks over high heat on one side for about 3 minutes. If flames flare up, douse them with water. Turn and grill on other side for 3 to 4 minutes. A meat thermometer should read 125°F for medium-rare, about 7 minutes total. Remove steaks to a cutting board. Tent with foil and let rest for 10 minutes to seal in juices. Slice steaks diagonally into 4 or 5 slices each.

TO PLATE: Put 4 potato halves next to each other on one side of 4 small plates. Put 2 onion halves next to potatoes. Arrange steak strips close together in center. Spoon a ribbon of Roquefort sauce across meat. Drizzle with balsamic vinegar and olive oil. Garnish with a sprig of parsley.

MAKES 4 SERVINGS

Asparagus Salad
with manchego cheese and serrano ham

This refreshing salad is a tribute to Spain. Manchego, Spain's most famous cheese, is so named because it is made only from the milk of Manchego sheep that graze the Spanish plains of La Mancha. For a delicious spring salad, pair this rich golden cheese with smoky Serrano ham, tender asparagus and leafy greens and dress it with a Spanish sherry vinaigrette. At Va de Vi we make this salad with white and green asparagus, but all green works well, too.

COUNTDOWN

Up to 2 days ahead
• Make vinaigrette and refrigerate.

Up to 4 hours ahead
• Cook asparagus. Leave at room temperature.

TIPS:

• To slice cheese paper thin, use a vegetable peeler.

• Asparagus can be grilled over high heat instead of blanched.

• White asparagus is sheltered from sunlight, so it doesn't develop the chlorophyll that turns it green. If using white asparagus, peel the stalks with a vegetable peeler. Tie them into a separate bundle from the green because they will take a little longer to cook.

INGREDIENTS

SPANISH SHERRY VINAIGRETTE

2 tablespoons coarsely chopped shallots
2 tablespoons Spanish sherry vinegar
½ cup extra virgin olive oil, divided
1 teaspoon sea salt
⅛ teaspoon freshly ground pepper

1 pound asparagus spears
2 heads baby greens such as lolla rossa and oakleaf, washed, trimmed and separated
4 ounces Spanish Manchego cheese, thinly sliced
4 ounces Serrano ham, thinly sliced

TO MAKE VINAIGRETTE: In a blender, blend shallots, vinegar and ¼ cup oil. With the motor running, slowly pour remaining ¼ cup oil through opening in top. Cover with a towel while pouring; it will splatter. Mix in sea salt and pepper. Use immediately or refrigerate. Mix well before using. Yields 1 cup.

TO COOK ASPARAGUS: Break off woody ends of 2 asparagus spears and cut remaining spears the same size. Tie into a bundle. In a wide saucepan, bring 4 to 5 inches of water to a boil. Add asparagus and cook uncovered for 2 to 4 minutes or until tender, but still crisp. Transfer to a bowl of ice water to stop the asparagus from cooking. Slice bottom inch of asparagus into thin rounds. Slice tops in half lengthwise.

TO ASSEMBLE SALAD: Put salad greens into a bowl. Add asparagus and toss with as much vinaigrette as desired. Divide between shallow soup bowls. Top with cheese and ham.

MAKES 4 SERVINGS

Grilled Pork Satay
with spicy peanut sauce

This is a great example of how I mix and match sauces. The pork is marinated in the same coconut milk mixture that is used for the Grilled Tiger Prawn Satay (page 78). On the grill, it is thickly coated with the Spicy Peanut Sauce I use to dress Chinese Noodles with Grilled Chicken Breasts (page 52). Crisp slices of pickled cucumber, cool papaya salad and pungent fukujin zuke (pickled vegetables) are terrific accompaniments to the richly glazed pork.

INGREDIENTS

1 recipe Pickled Cucumbers (page 165)
1 recipe Spicy Peanut Sauce, divided
 (page 158)
1 recipe Green Papaya Salad (page 148)

THAI COCONUT MILK MARINADE

1 stalk lemongrass, coarsely chopped
1 tablespoon finely chopped garlic

1 can (13.5 ounces) coconut milk
2 tablespoons Asian fish sauce
 (nuac mam)

1 pound boneless pork shoulder butt

PRESENTATION

Fukujin zuke (pickled vegetables)
Sprigs of cilantro

TO MAKE MARINADE: In a bowl, whisk together lemongrass, garlic, coconut milk and fish sauce.

TO MARINATE: Slice pork across the grain into approximately ¼-inch-thick slices. Because of the irregularity of the meat, the pieces will not be the same size. Aim for pieces 3 inches long and 1 inch wide. Place pork in a plastic zipper bag, pour 1½ cups marinade over and toss to coat. Refrigerate for a minimum of 6 hours or preferably overnight, tossing bag occasionally.

TO GRILL: Soak twelve 10-inch-long bamboo skewers in water for at least 30 minutes. Remove pork from marinade, leaving excess marinade on meat. Discard marinade. Thread pork onto skewers. Oil grill grate and prepare coals or preheat gas grill to high. Grill over medium heat, turning, for 15 to 20 minutes, or until medium (about 135°F). Generously coat meat with 1 cup peanut sauce. Grill, turning and basting generously, until outside is charred and inside is pink. Remove from heat and let rest 5 minutes for juices to settle.

TO PLATE: Toss papaya salad with dressing. Spoon a mound of papaya salad onto the center of 6 dinner plates. Arrange several pickled cucumbers next to it. Cross 2 satays over salad. Sprinkle with several pieces of fukujin zuke. Top with a sprig of cilantro and drizzle with ¼ cup peanut sauce. Reserve remaining 1¼ cup peanut sauce for another use.

MAKES 6 SERVINGS

COUNTDOWN

As far ahead as deired
• Make pickled cucumber.

Up to 2 weeks ahead
• Make peanut sauce and refrigerate. Bring to room temperature; whisk before using.

1 day ahead
• Make marinade; marinate pork in refrigerator.

4 hours ahead
• Make papaya salad and dressing; refrigerate separately.

1 hour ahead
• Prepare coals.
• Soak bamboo skewers in water.

25 minutes before serving
• Grill pork.

Just before serving
• Toss papaya salad with dressing.

Sautéed Savoy Spinach
with lemon, garlic and tomatoes

I call this dish thirty-second spinach because if you cook it any longer it will be overcooked. Savoy is the spinach of choice because it doesn't wilt as quickly and retains its texture better than baby spinach. If you substitute baby spinach, you'll need to make this a twenty-five second dish.

TIPS:

• It is important to have all ingredients ready before beginning to cook.
• Toy box tomatoes are available in the summer; grape tomatoes are available in the spring, fall and winter.

INGREDIENTS

2 tablespoons vegetable or olive oil
2 teaspoons finely chopped garlic
10 to 12 ounces savoy spinach
1 tablespoon fresh lemon juice

8 to 12 toy box or grape tomatoes, at room temperature
¼ teaspoon sea salt

TO PREPARE SPINACH: In a wok or large skillet, heat oil over high heat until almost smoking. Working quickly, stir in garlic and half the spinach. Toss and stir until spinach begins to wilt, and then stir in remainder. Quickly stir in lemon juice; spinach will reduce to about half. Stir in tomatoes. Season with ¼ teaspoon salt and pepper to taste. Serve immediately.

MAKES 4 SERVINGS

Risotto with Grilled Porcini Mushrooms,

sweet onions, fava beans and pecorino romano

This is one of our most popular vegetarian dishes. It represents the beauty of using the best ingredients at their optimum harvest: fresh porcini mushrooms, sweet onions and green garlic. Grilling the vegetables adds a subtle smoky flavor. This risotto has so many great flavors that you can omit the cheese and turn it into a delicious vegan entrée.

TIPS:

*   Supplement fresh porcini mushrooms with dried because the dried have a more intense flavor.
*   If you can't find porcini, use chanterelles or morels.
*   Fava beans, also called broad beans, are shelled and then the tough outer skin needs to be peeled. A good substitute for fava beans is shelled edamame.
*   Stir risotto gently to avoid breaking the grains.
*   Shred Pecorino cheese on the medium holes of a grater. I use a medium ribbon grater by Microplane.

COUNTDOWN

Up to 1 day ahead
• Soak dried porcini.

Up to 4½ hours ahead
• Prepare coals.

Up to 4 hours ahead
• Shell, cook and peel fava beans; leave covered at room temperature.
• Grill onion, garlic and fresh porcini mushrooms; leave covered at room temperature.
• Begin risotto.
• Make fried sage leaves.

20 minutes ahead
• Finish risotto.

INGREDIENTS

1 recipe Crispy Fried Sage Leaves
   (page 162)

VEGETABLES

¼ cup dried porcini mushrooms
½ sweet onion, peeled
2 stalks green garlic
½ cup fresh porcini mushrooms, rinsed
   and dried
½ cup fresh fava beans, shelled

RISOTTO

3 tablespoons extra virgin olive oil
1 tablespoon finely chopped garlic

¼ cup finely chopped shallots
1 cup Italian Arborio rice
1 cup dry white wine, such as
   sauvignon blanc
1 tablespoon julienned fresh tarragon
½ cup shredded Pecorino
   Romano cheese

PRESENTATION

Porcini oil or extra virgin olive oil
Shredded Pecorino Romano cheese
Coarsely ground black pepper

TO PREPARE VEGETABLES: Rinse dried mushrooms in water several times to remove any grit. Put them into a bowl and add 1 cup of hot water. Put a smaller bowl on top to submerge them in the water. Soak for at least one hour or overnight. Drain through a fine strainer, reserving the liquid. Grill sweet onion, green garlic and fresh porcini until lightly charred. Cool. Finely chop the onion and garlic and slice the fresh mushrooms . Blanch fava beans in boiling water for 2 to 3 minutes or until outsides turn pale and they crack open slightly. Drain and run under cold water to stop the cooking. Pinch the beans to slide them out of their skins. Cover vegetables and keep at room temperature.

TO BEGIN RISOTTO: In a 12-inch skillet, heat olive oil over medium heat until hot. Add garlic and shallots and sauté until translucent, 2 minutes. Add rice and stir until all grains are coated, 1 minute. Add reserved porcini liquid and simmer, stirring constantly, until almost all the liquid is absorbed. Add wine.

Simmer, stirring, until most, but not all, of the moisture is absorbed and grains are beginning to get creamy. Risotto can be made ahead to this point. Cover and set aside at room temperature. Reheat before continuing.

TO FINISH RISOTTO: Add 1 cup water to risotto and simmer over medium heat, stirring often, until almost all liquid is absorbed. Add 1 more cup of water and simmer, stirring, until liquid is absorbed and grains are almost tender. Stir in fava beans, sweet onion, green garlic, and dried and fresh porcini. Season with sea salt and pepper. Risotto is done when the rice is creamy and the grains are soft, but there is slight pressure in the center when bitten into. Stir in tarragon and cheese.

TO PLATE: Divide risotto between 6 small plates. Drizzle with oil. Sprinkle with cheese and pepper. Top with fried sage leaves.

MAKES 6 SERVINGS

Chinese Noodles

with grilled chicken breasts in spicy peanut sauce

In this popular dish, the noodles are served at room temperature topped with warm sliced chicken breast. Because the noodles can be prepared ahead, it makes a terrific party dish for a large group. It's filling, so a little goes a long way.

INGREDIENTS

1 recipe Green Onion Curls
   (page 164)
1 recipe Spicy Peanut Sauce (page 158)

CHILI SAUCE WITH HONEY

¾ cup vegetable oil
1½ tablespoons lemon juice
1 tablespoon chili sauce with garlic
1 tablespoon honey
1 teaspoon soy sauce
1 clove garlic, minced
2 boneless, skinless chicken breast halves
   (4 ounces total),
   tenderloins removed

NOODLES AND VEGETABLES

6 ounces Asian fresh or dried egg or
   water noodles
2 teaspoons vegetable oil
¼ teaspoon sesame oil
¼ hot house cucumber, unpeeled
   and julienned
1 carrot, peeled and julienned

PRESENTATION

4 to 6 sprigs of cilantro

COUNTDOWN

Up to 2 weeks ahead
• Make peanut sauce and
  refrigerate.

Up to 1 week ahead
• Make chili sauce and
  refrigerate.

Up to 4 hours ahead
• Boil noodles and toss with
  cucumbers and carrots. Cover
  at room temperature.
• Bring peanut sauce and chili
  sauce to room temperature.
• Make green onion curls.

1 hour ahead
• Marinate chicken.
• Prepare coals.

25 minutes ahead
• Grill chicken breasts.

Just before serving
• Toss noodles with
  peanut sauce.

TO MAKE CHILI SAUCE: In a medium bowl, whisk all chili sauce ingredients until blended. Use immediately or refrigerate. Bring to room temperature before using. Makes 1 cup.

TO MARINATE CHICKEN: Put chicken into a plastic zipper bag. Add chili sauce; toss to coat. Marinate for 1 hour at room temperature, tossing once.

TO PREPARE NOODLES AND VEGETABLES: Bring a pot of salted water to a boil. Add noodles and cook until al dente, 3 minutes for fresh, 5 minutes for dried. Drain and run under cold water until cool. Transfer to a bowl. Add vegetable oil and sesame oil; toss to coat. Stir in cucumbers and carrots.

TO GRILL CHICKEN: Oil grill grate and prepare coals or preheat gas grill. Grill over medium heat until underside has deep brown grill marks, 6 to 8 minutes. Turn and continue grilling until cooked through, 6 to 8 more minutes. Chicken is done when thickest part is opaque. Let rest 5 minutes; slice thinly on the diagonal.

TO PLATE: Toss noodles with as much peanut sauce as desired. Mound noodles onto the center of 4 small plates. Top with slices of chicken. Drizzle with peanut sauce. Top with green onion curls and a sprig of cilantro.

MAKES 4 TO 6 SERVINGS

Seared Alaskan Halibut
with thai red curry sauce and strawberry papaya-mint relish

Growing up in Hawaii allowed me to experience the flavor of truly delicious papaya. Their reddish-orange or pink flesh differentiates strawberry papayas from others, but any ripe Hawaiian papaya can be used in the relish. I like to cool the spices in curry with the sweetness of papaya.

TIP:

• At Va de Vi we use Alaskan halibut, but in this recipe any local halibut will work.

COUNTDOWN

Up to 2 weeks ahead
• Make curry sauce and refrigerate.

Up to 3 days ahead
• Make papaya relish and refrigerate. Stir before serving.

1 hour ahead
• Bring relish to room temperature.

5 minutes ahead
• Reheat curry sauce.
• Cook halibut.

INGREDIENTS

¾ cup Thai Red Curry Sauce (page 159)

STRAWBERRY PAPAYA-MINT RELISH

3 tablespoons diced red onion

2 tablespoon aji-mirin

2 tablespoons bottled sweet red chili sauce

2 tablespoons julienned fresh mint

1 cup diced strawberry papaya (1 fresh papaya)

FISH

1 tablespoon vegetable oil

4 halibut filets, skinned, cut 1 inch thick (about 3 ounces each)

PRESENTATION

1 teaspoon fukujin zuke (pickled vegetables)

2 teaspoons julienned Thai basil

4 small sprigs cilantro

TO MAKE MINT RELISH: In a medium bowl, whisk onion, aji-mirin, chili sauce and mint until blended. Stir in papaya. Season with sea salt and pepper to taste. Refrigerate for at least 1 hour. Makes 1¼ cups.

TO COOK FISH: In a 12-inch skillet, preferably non-stick, heat oil over high heat until almost smoking. Season one side of halibut with sea salt and pepper. Sear for 1½ to 2 minutes. Turn and sear other side about 1½ minutes or until cooked through.

TO PLATE: Spread enough curry sauce on the bottom of 4 shallow soup bowls to form a pool 3 inches in diameter. Place halibut fillet in center. Top with a spoonful of relish, a few pieces of fukujin zuke, a sprinkling of basil and a sprig of cilantro.

MAKES 4 SERVINGS

Grilled Rosemary and Garlic-Crusted Lamb Chops
with ratatouille and yukon gold mashed potatoes

When I think of lamb, I think of rosemary and garlic so I use generous amounts of both in this marinade. In my opinion, if a marinade doesn't have lots of flavor, there is no reason to use it. This recipe is a simple combination of marinated grilled lamb chops resting on a bed of mashed potatoes and lightly sautéed eggplant, squash and peppers.

TIPS:
- To quickly remove rosemary stems from leaves, squeeze the top of the stem and run your fingers down the stem to separate the leaves as you go.
- Ask the butcher to French the bones, which means to cut the bottom part of the meat so the bone is exposed.
- Consider using New Zealand lamb, which is smaller and can be more tender than domestic lamb.

INGREDIENTS

1 recipe Yukon Gold Mashed Potatoes (page 153)
½ recipe Fresh Ratatouille (page 147)

ROSEMARY GARLIC MARINADE
1 cup extra virgin olive oil
1 cup fresh rosemary, stemmed
1 shallot, peeled
6 cloves garlic, peeled
2 dried or fresh bay leaves
1 tablespoon juniper berries
1 tablespoon black peppercorns

One 8-rib rack of lamb (1¼ to 1½ pounds), bones Frenched

LAMB JUS
1 tablespoon butter
4 garlic cloves, peeled and chopped
2 shallots, peeled and chopped
4 stems fresh rosemary, coarsely chopped
¾ cup dry red wine, such as cabernet sauvignon
1 tablespoon black peppercorns
⅓ cup lamb demi-glace dissolved in ½ cup water

TO MAKE MARINADE: In a blender or food processor, process all ingredients until blended. Marinade may be used immediately or refrigerated overnight. Bring to room temperature and whisk well before using. Makes about 1½ cups.

TO PREPARE LAMB: Cut between bones to make 4 servings of 2 chops each. Score fat side of chops by cutting thin diagonal cuts on the surface. Turn ribs over and make shallow cuts on the meat between the bones.

TO MARINATE: Place lamb in a plastic zipper bag. Pour marinade over, tossing to coat. Refrigerate overnight, turning occasionally. Bring to room temperature in marinade 1 hour before grilling.

TO MAKE LAMB JUS: In a small saucepan over medium heat, melt butter. Stir in garlic and shallots and sauté until translucent and aromatic, about 2 minutes. Add remaining ingredients. Simmer over medium-

COUNTDOWN

1 day ahead
- Make marinade and marinate lamb.

Up to 1 day ahead
- Make lamb jus and refrigerate.

5 hours ahead
- Salt and drain eggplant for ratatouille.

4 hours ahead
- Make ratatouille.
- Make mashed potatoes.

1 hour ahead
- Bring lamb to room temperature.
- Prepare coals.

40 minutes ahead
- Grill lamb.
- Finish ratatouille.

low heat until it is a rich brown color and reduced to ¾ cup, about 40 minutes. Strain and return to saucepan. Reheat before serving. Season with sea salt and pepper to taste.

TO GRILL LAMB: Oil grill grate and prepare coals or preheat gas grill to high. When coals are ready, decrease heat on one side to medium by rearranging coals. Remove chops from marinade (do not remove excess marinade from meat) and season with sea salt and pepper. Place fat side down on hot side of grill. Grill until meat is charred, about 3 minutes. If flames flare up, douse them with water. Turn and char bone side down, 2 minutes. Remove to other side of grill over medium heat to finish cooking. Grill, turning occasionally, until medium-rare, 125°F on a meat thermometer, about 10 minutes total. Remove from heat to a cutting board. Tent with foil and let sit for 10 minutes for the juices to settle. Carve into individual chops.

TO PLATE: Spoon lamb jus into the bottom of 4 shallow soup bowls. Spoon mashed potatoes into the back half of bowls. Place ratatouille on top and around potatoes. Arrange 2 chops standing in an 'X' across potatoes and ratatouille.

MAKES 4 SERVINGS

Ratatouille in Grilled Radicchio Cups

Although my ratatouille is more attractive than most, spooning it into grilled purple radicchio cups adds a nice jolt of color.

INGREDIENTS

½ recipe Fresh Ratatouille (page 147)
1 head radicchio (8 ounces), cut in half
    through the core

1 tablespoon extra virgin olive oil
PRESENTATION
Julienned basil

TO GRILL RADICCHIO: Oil grill rack and heat coals or preheat gas grill on high. Rub cut side of radicchio with olive oil. Place cut side down on grill. Grill over high heat, turning, until inside and outside are lightly charred, about 4 minutes.

TO PLATE: Remove leaves from radicchio and place one outer leaf or 2 smaller leaves on 6 small plates. Open them out like a cup and spoon ratatouille into them. Sprinkle ratatouille with basil.

MAKES 4 TO 5 SIDE DISH SERVINGS

COUNTDOWN

Up to 5 hours ahead
• Salt and drain eggplant for ratatouille.

Up to 4 hours ahead
• Cook vegetables for ratatouille.

Up to 1½ hours ahead
• Prepare coals.

Up to 1 hour ahead
• Grill radicchio.

Huckleberry Bread Pudding
with crème anglaise and huckleberry sauce

Not all bread puddings are created equal. This one has enough custard to keep the bread cubes suspended and is scattered throughout with deep blue huckleberries. Huckleberries are often mistaken for blueberries, but they are shinier with a deeper color and have a tangier, more complex taste. The pudding is accented with two sauces, one made with huckleberries and the other a velvety custard.

COUNTDOWN

Up to 2 days ahead
• Make huckleberry sauce.
• Make crème anglaise.

1 to 2 days ahead
• Dry bread cubes.

Up to 6 hours ahead
• Make custard for pudding and refrigerate. Whisk well before using.

2½ hours ahead
• Assemble and bake pudding.

TIPS:

• Fresh or frozen wild blueberries may be substituted for the huckleberries with delicious results. If using frozen berries, do not defrost them.

• If you don't have time to let the bread cubes dry out at room temperature for 1 to 2 days, you can bake them at 200°F for 90 minutes, tossing every 30 minutes until lightly toasted.

• You may find it unusual to bake the pudding covered with plastic wrap and foil. The plastic wrap makes a tighter seal and helps the pudding steam. At the low oven temperature, the foil protects the wrap and keeps it from melting.

• I like to serve the pudding one hour after baking it, although it can be made earlier and reheated at 300°F for 10 minutes.

• To match the photo, cut out rounds of bread pudding with a 2-inch biscuit cutter like we do at Va de Vi.

INGREDIENTS

1 recipe Huckleberry Sauce (page 158)
1 recipe Vanilla Bean Crème Anglaise (page 160)
1 loaf (16 ounces) unsliced challah (egg bread) or brioche
4 large eggs

2 egg yolks
1 cup sugar
3 cups heavy cream
1½ teaspoons vanilla extract
Pinch of sea salt
2 tablespoons Grand Marnier
1 cup huckleberries

TO PREPARE BREAD: Cut off ends of bread and discard. Cut bread with crust into 1-inch cubes. Put onto a rimmed baking sheet and let dry uncovered at room temperature for one to two days, tossing occasionally.

TO PREPARE CUSTARD: In a bowl, whisk together whole eggs, yolks, sugar, cream, vanilla, salt and Grand Marnier until blended. Custard may be used immediately or refrigerated. Whisk before using.

TO ASSEMBLE PUDDING: Spray or grease a 7 by 11-inch baking dish. Put bread cubes in a very large bowl. Pour approximately half the custard over and toss to coat all surfaces. Set bread aside for 15 to 25 minutes, stirring occasionally until very soft and almost mushy. Pour one layer of bread in bottom of prepared dish. Sprinkle with ½ cup berries. Top with remaining bread and remaining ½ cup berries. Whisk reserved custard and pour reserved custard over the top. Press on bread with your hands or a spatula to push it down into custard. Cover with plastic wrap and foil.

TO BAKE: Preheat oven to 300°F. The pudding needs to cook in a water bath (bain-marie) to retain its creamy consistency. Choose a 3- to-4 inch-deep roasting pan that the baking dish can fit in comfortably. Place pudding in pan and place in oven. Pour enough boiling water into outside pan to come halfway up the pudding dish. Bake for 60 minutes. A knife inserted near the center will come out lightly coated with custard. Cool for 30 to 60 minutes before serving. Pudding is best served warm.

TO PLATE: Spoon enough crème anglaise sauce to cover bottom of dessert plate. Spoon bread pudding into center. Top pudding with enough huckleberry sauce so that it runs down the sides and pools onto the crème anglaise. Serve immediately.

MAKES 8 SERVINGS

Va De Vi Cheese Tray

Knowledge and organization go into making a good cheese tray. At Va de Vi I like to feature three cheeses, each from a different country, usually from the United States, Italy, France or Spain and each having different characteristics, such as a soft cheese, a semi-hard cheese and one with a bold flavor.

TIPS:

• For a cheese course that is part of the meal, a selection of three cheeses will suffice.

• Allow one-half to one ounce of cheese per person.

• Remove cheese from the refrigerator 60 to 90 minutes before serving.

• Tell your guests what the cheeses are and that they should begin with the mildest and work toward the strongest.

HERE IS A SELECTION OF THE MOST POPULAR CHEESES SERVED IN THE RESTAURANT. CHOOSE ONE FROM EACH CATEGORY.

Cheese Number 1: Soft cheese

MT. TAM – A smooth and creamy cheese with a mellow, earthy flavor, made with pasteurized organic cow's milk by Cow Girl Creamery in California.

HUMBOLDT FOG – It's center layer of vegetable ash and exterior of ash and white mold makes it reminiscent of early morning fog. The white pate develops a soft runny edge with age. This goat's milk cheese is from a farm called Cypress Grove Chèvre in California.

BRILLAT-SAVARIN – Named for Jean Anthelme Brillat-Savarin, a famous food writer in 18th century France, this soft, white-crusted cow's milk cheese is slightly acidic with a tender or creamy consistency.

PIERRE ROBERT – Luxuriously rich and creamy, this French cheese ripens to a perfect buttery texture with a tangy bite not often found in this style of cheese.

Cheese Number 2: Semi-hard cheese

CACIOTTA DEI BOSCHI – This is an elegant table cheese made from scarce Roman sheep's milk, rare black truffle shavings and bits of porcini mushrooms. It is quite tangy, sharp and highly aromatic.

SOTTOCENERE AROMATIZZATO AL TARTUFO – Consisting of soft, solid Italian cow's milk cheese with flakes of black truffles inside; after a short ripening, the surface undergoes a treatment with extra virgin olive oil, spices, (especially cinnamon) and natural truffle flavoring.

BERMUDA TRIANGLE – From Cyprus Grove Chèvre in California, this double rind goat's milk cheese was awarded first place at the American Cheese Society judging for the best American- made international style cheese.

Cheese Number 3: Highly flavored cheese

MURCIA AL VINO – This wine-bathed goat's milk cheese is made in the Murcia region of Spain. Red wine deeply tints the cheese, giving the rind its characteristic burgundy color and imparting a strong floral bouquet.

GORGONZOLA DOLCE – From Italy's Lombardy region comes the most imitated blue cheese in the world. Many cheeses falsely claim to be gorgonzola, but they always leave you singing the blues. Almost spreadable, Gorgonzola Dolce is supple and luxurious with an unmistakable tangy creaminess. Its pale white interior is laced with streaks of blue, giving it a striking appearance to match its piquant flavor.

PECORINO UBRIACO – This stunning wine-soaked pecorino caciotta hails from Tuscany. The rich, flavorful and salty taste of pecorino is a great combination with robust cabernet sauvignon wine. This aromatic cheese is typically eaten as a table cheese and is served with the edible rind.

PRESENTATION: On the plate or tray with the cheeses, arrange small servings of Marcona almonds, quince paste, Australian crispbread (Falwasser) or slices of baguette, slices of gala apple, blood oranges or peaches and a sprig of lavender.

Summer

There comes a time in every grapes' life when it needs to leave behind the carefree days of childhood and transition to a life of productivity and maturity. That time is summer. Up until mid-summer a grape lives the relaxing life of a small green berry, slowly getting bigger and fatter. All of this soon changes. At a certain point the growth slows, the sugar content starts to rapidly increase, the flesh softens and the skins start to transform. If it's a white grape variety, the skin transforms from a soft, dark green to a translucent golden color. If it's a red variety then the skin changes from the same soft, dark green to a deep, dark purple/black. This change in color is called verasion and now the countdown to harvest has begun.

Summer is a great time for crisp and fruity wines; pretend you are in the south of France and try a dry rosé from the **Pink Pride – Dry Rosé** wines or dream of Australian beaches while having a glass of sauvignon blanc or any of the **Snappy - Juicy and Brisk** white wines. Grilling on the Fourth of July? Nothing goes better than a glass of a **Yummy – Jammy and Spicy** red like old vines zinfandel.

–Brendan Eliason

Summer is about grilling. Vegetables, especially corn, are delicious cooked on the grill. And, of course, summer is about tomatoes. Enjoy them in salads, relishes and even in a sorbet. Berries peak, as do the stone fruits, leading to wonderful crisps, cobblers and pies. Warm weather brings out the best in everything.

-Kelly Degala

Summer Recipes

Basil-Marinated Mozzarella
with heirloom tomatoes

COUNTDOWN

Up to 1 day ahead
• Marinate mozzarella.

2 hours ahead
• Bring mozzarella to room temperature.

In Italian this salad is called Caprese and there are as many variations as there are chefs. The difference between a ho-hum and a wow Caprese salad lies in the quality of the ingredients. You need the best Italian mozzarella, the ripest heirloom tomatoes, the finest extra virgin olive oil and an aged Aceto Balsamico Tradizionale di Modena.

TIPS:

• If the heirloom tomatoes you purchase are not grown in a hot house, you must be sure to wash them very well. If they are grown in pastures or near farms, there is a chance they could be contaminated.

• Use a variety of colors and types of heirloom tomatoes. There are so many to choose from. Some I recommend are Green Zebra, Beefsteak, Mr. Stripey, Brandywine, Bush Celebrity and Big Boy.

INGREDIENTS

BASIL MARINADE

1½ cups loosely-packed basil leaves (about 1 ounce)
½ cup extra virgin olive oil
2 tablespoons grated Parmesano Reggiano cheese
¼ teaspoon sea salt
¼ teaspoon freshly ground pepper

8 ounces fresh Italian mozzarella, sliced ⅛ inch thick
1 pound heirloom tomatoes, cored and sliced into ¼-inch-thick rounds
2 ounces fresh basil leaves
Extra virgin olive oil
Aged balsamic vinegar

TO MAKE BASIL MARINADE: In a food processor, process all marinade ingredients until pureed.

TO MARINATE MOZZARELLA: Arrange slices of mozzarella overlapping slightly in a pie plate. Pour marinade over. Cover and marinate at least 1 hour at room temperature or overnight in the refrigerator. When ready to use, remove mozzarella from marinade, but do not wipe off.

TO PLATE: Place a slice of tomato off-center on a dinner plate. Place a slice of mozzarella slightly overlapping the tomato. Press a whole basil leaf on mozzarella. Repeat, alternating colors of tomatoes, slices of cheese and basil leaves to make a circle. With your hands, press the circle towards the center of the plate. Drizzle with olive oil and balsamic vinegar. Sprinkle with sea salt and pepper.

MAKES 4 SERVINGS

Niçoise Salad
Va de Vi Style

This salad epitomizes the small plate concept. It makes a delicious appetizer, a first course salad or an entrée. The salad consists of several components, each made separately and then attractively arranged on plates. I think of this as 'orchestrating' the plate.

TIPS:

- It is very important to purchase sashimi grade #1 tuna. If it has any blood or skin on it, remove it before cooking.
- Instead of searing the tuna, it may be grilled over high heat for 30 to 60 seconds per side.

INGREDIENTS

½ recipe Pickled Onions (page 166), drained
1 recipe Dijon Mustard Vinaigrette (page 156)

FINGERLING POTATOES
10 sprigs fresh thyme
4 to 5 fingerling potatoes, scrubbed and dried
1 tablespoon extra virgin olive oil
Sea salt

TUNA
12 to 16 ounces sashimi grade #1 tuna, cut into four 1-inch-thick steaks

1 tablespoon extra virgin olive oil
Freshly ground pepper

SALAD
2 hard boiled eggs, shelled and quartered lengthwise
8 whole white anchovies or good quality black anchovies
16 pitted Niçoise olives
4 teaspoons capers, drained and rinsed
3 heads baby leafy greens, such as lolla rossa, tango and oak leaf, washed, trimmed and separated

COUNTDOWN

As far ahead as desired
- Make pickled onions.

Up to 3 days ahead
- Make mustard vinaigrette and refrigerate.

Up to 1 day ahead
- Boil eggs and refrigerate.

Up to 4 hours ahead
- Bake potatoes and keep covered at room temperature.

Just before serving
- Sear tuna and slice.

TO BAKE POTATOES: Preheat oven to 400°F. Put thyme sprigs in pie plate or shallow baking pan. Add potatoes; sprinkle with olive oil and salt. Toss to coat. Cover with foil. Bake 30 minutes or until almost tender. Remove foil and continue to bake uncovered for 10 minutes or until tender. Cool to room temperature. Slice crosswise.

TO COOK TUNA: Heat a large skillet over high heat until very hot. Brush both sides of tuna with oil and sprinkle with pepper. Place in pan; it should sizzle and smoke. Sear for 45 to 60 seconds until bottom is golden. Turn and sear for 30 to 45 seconds. Remove from heat. Slice ¼ inch thick.

TO PLATE: Fan potato slices around center of 4 plates. Arrange separate groups of eggs, anchovies, olives and capers around plate. Toss lettuce leaves with as much vinaigrette as desired and arrange in center of plate. Overlap tuna slices on lettuce. Top with a spoonful of pickled onions. Grind pepper over and drizzle with additional dressing.

MAKES 4 SERVINGS

Grilled Kalbi Flat Iron Steak

with green papaya salad

Kalbi refers to a popular Korean barbecue dish. The marinade is made with ingredients you most likely have in your kitchen and is so versatile it complements almost any meat or poultry. You'll receive raves when you serve these tender, juicy steaks with their crusty, caramelized exterior.

TIPS:

- You will have more marinade than you need, but in addition to marinating, it is also used for basting and glazing the steaks.
- Steaks may be broiled instead of grilled.

INGREDIENTS

1 recipe Green Papaya Salad
   (page 148)
1 recipe Kimchee (page 148) or jarred
   kimchee
1 recipe Green Onion Curls
   (page 164)

KALBI MARINADE

2 cups soy sauce
½ cup vegetable oil
2 teaspoons sesame oil
2 tablespoons finely chopped ginger
2 tablespoons honey

2 cups golden brown sugar, packed
¼ cup toasted sesame seeds
2 green onions with tops, thinly sliced
2 teaspoons freshly ground pepper
2 teaspoons crushed red chili flakes

16 ounces flat iron steak, about 1¼
   inch thick, cut into
   4 (4 ounce) portions

PRESENTATION

4 sprigs cilantro or basil

COUNTDOWN

Up to 2 weeks ahead
- Make marinade.

Up to 1 week ahead
- Make kimchee, if using homemade.

1 day ahead
- Marinate steaks.

4 hours ahead
- Marinate steaks at room temperature.
- Make green onion curls.
- Make papaya salad and dressing; refrigerate separately.

1 hour ahead
- Prepare coals.

25 minutes before serving
- Grill steaks.

Just before serving
- Toss papaya salad with dressing.

TO MAKE MARINADE: Measure all ingredients into a deep bowl and whisk until blended. Use immediately or refrigerate. Bring to room temperature and whisk well before using. Makes 4 cups.

TO MARINATE: Put steaks into a plastic zipper bag. Pour 2 cups of the marinade over steaks. Reserve remaining 2 cups for basting and glazing. Refrigerate steaks overnight, turning once or twice. Bring steaks to room temperature in marinade for 4 hours before grilling.

TO GRILL: Oil grill grate and prepare coals or preheat gas grill to high. Remove steaks from marinade; discard used marinade. Season with sea salt and pepper. Grill over medium heat, basting occasionally with 1 cup of the reserved marinade, until underside is deep brown and grill marks appear, 4 to 6 minutes. Turn and grill, basting occasionally, 4 to 6 more minutes for medium-rare, 125°F on an instant read thermometer. Watch carefully, because the high sugar content of the marinade tends to burn easily. Transfer to a cutting board, tent with foil and let rest 10 minutes for the juices to settle. Slice diagonally against the grain.

TO PLATE: Spoon a bed of papaya salad onto 4 small plates. Arrange steak slices overlapping on salad. Glaze with remaining 1 cup of reserved marinade. Top with kimchee, green onion curls and a sprig of cilantro or basil.

MAKES 4 SERVINGS

Hoisin-Glazed Baby Back Pork Ribs

For succulent ribs with meat that falls off the bone, I cook them in three stages. First they are boiled, which helps break down the meat's tough fibers. Then they are baked at a low temperature. For the final step they are either baked or grilled. To obtain the layering of flavors, I first bake them in a thin spicy chili sauce and then baste them with a thick, sweet and tangy Asian barbeque sauce. These are everything great ribs should be: tender, caramelized and 'finger-lickin' sticky. Be sure to offer lots of napkins.

INGREDIENTS

1 recipe Green Papaya Salad
(page 148)
1 recipe Hoisin Barbecue Sauce
(page 156)

CHILI SAUCE WITH HONEY

¾ cup vegetable oil
1½ tablespoons lemon juice
1 tablespoon chili sauce with garlic
1 tablespoon honey
1 teaspoon soy sauce
1 clove garlic, minced

RIBS

2 racks baby back pork ribs
(2 to 2½ pounds each)
2 green onions, sliced, including tops
About 2 inches fresh ginger, peeled and
coarsely chopped
1 head garlic, smashed and cloves
coarsely chopped (skin and all)

PRESENTATION

Toasted sesame seeds

COUNTDOWN

Up to 2 weeks ahead
• Make barbecue sauce and refrigerate.

Up to 1 week ahead
• Make chili sauce and refrigerate.

Up to 6 hours ahead
• Boil ribs, drain and leave covered at room temperature.
• Bring chili sauce to room temperature.

Up to 4 hours ahead
• Bake ribs with chili sauce. Leave covered at room temperature.
• Make papaya salad and dressing; refrigerate separately.

25 minutes before serving
• Bake or grill ribs.

Just before serving
• Toss salad with dressing.

TO MAKE CHILI SAUCE: In a medium bowl, whisk all ingredients together until blended. Use immediately or refrigerate up to 1 week. Bring to room temperature before using. Makes 1 cup.

TO BOIL RIBS: Place ribs in a large wide saucepan, such as a Dutch oven. If they don't fit, cut the racks in half. Add green onions, ginger and garlic. Add enough water to barely cover ribs. Cover pan and bring to a boil over high heat. Reduce heat and boil slowly until meat begins to pull away from bones, 40 to 50 minutes. Drain. Cool slightly.

TO BAKE: Preheat oven to 275°F. Line a sheet pan or shallow roasting pan with a double thickness of foil; set a roasting rack in pan and spray with nonstick coating. Smear both sides of ribs generously with chili sauce. Place bone side down on rack. Bake for 45 minutes, basting occasionally.

FINAL BAKING OR GRILLING: If ribs were made ahead, bake or grill until hot. Generously brush meat side only with barbecue sauce.

TO BAKE: Preheat oven to 325°F. Return ribs to rack. Bake for 10 minutes or until deeply browned and bubbling. Baste with barbecue sauce and bake for 5 to 10 more minutes, until ribs are glazed and caramelized.

TO GRILL: Oil grill grate and prepare coals or preheat gas grill on high. Grill over medium heat for 5 to 7 minutes or until meat is deeply browned and grill marks appear. Baste with barbecue sauce and grill for 5 to 7 more minutes, until glazed and caramelized. Watch carefully, they burn easily. Let rest 5 minutes and cut between ribs.

TO PLATE: Spoon a small bed of salad on the bottom of 4 small plates. Place 2 ribs on salad. Arrange 2 ribs on top crosswise and 2 more crosswise again. Glaze lightly with barbeque sauce and sprinkle with sesame seeds.

MAKES 4 SERVINGS (6 RIBS EACH)

Grilled Asparagus
with remoulàde sauce and crispy fried shallots

This is a dynamite combination. Smoky asparagus spears are coated with a tangy caper mayonnaise and topped off with crunchy fried shallot rings.

INGREDIENTS

½ recipe Remoulàde Sauce (page 157)
1 recipe Crispy Fried Shallots
   (page 162)
1 bunch asparagus spears
   (1 to 1¼ pounds)

1 tablespoon olive oil

PRESENTATION
Blood orange oil
Freshly ground pepper

TO GRILL ASPARAGUS: Break off woody ends of 2 asparagus spears and cut remaining spears the same size. Place in a bowl and toss with olive oil. Oil the grill grate and heat coals or preheat gas grill on high. Grill asparagus over medium heat, turning with tongs, until crisp tender and lightly charred. Asparagus can be served warm or at room temperature.

TO PLATE: Divide asparagus between 4 small plates. Spoon a dollop of sauce across the center. Sprinkle fried shallots over the sauce. Drizzle with orange oil and grind pepper over the top to taste.

MAKES 4 SERVINGS

COUNTDOWN

Up to 2 days ahead
• Make remoulàde sauce and refrigerate.

Up to 4 hours ahead
• Make fried shallots.

Up to 1½ hours ahead
• Prepare grill.

Up to 1 hour ahead
• Grill asparagus. Store at room temperature.

Grilled Tiger Prawn Satay
with thai red curry glaze

Foods marinated in coconut milk are a favorite with Va de Vi customers, especially when they are coated with a spicy curry sauce. I like to pair these succulent prawns with cool and crunchy cucumber pickles and fukujin zuke (pickled vegetables).

COUNTDOWN

As far ahead as desired
• Make pickled cucumber.

Up to 2 weeks ahead
• Make curry sauce and refrigerate.

30 minutes ahead
• Marinate prawns.
• Soak skewers in water.
• Prepare coals.

TIPS:

• Thai coconut milk marinade can also be used to marinate pork, chicken and fish, such as salmon and halibut. Marinate meats overnight in the refrigerator; marinate fish and seafood 30 minutes at room temperature.

• To serve as hors d'oeuvre, instead of coating the grilled prawns with the Thai Red Curry Sauce, put the warm sauce into a bowl and serve as a dip with the prawns.

INGREDIENTS

1 recipe Pickled Cucumber (page 165)
½ to ¾ cup Thai Red Curry Sauce
   (page 159)

THAI COCONUT MILK MARINADE

1 cup lemongrass, coarsely chopped
1 tablespoon finely chopped garlic
1 can (13.5 ounces) coconut milk

2 tablespoons Asian fish sauce
   (nuac mam)

16 tiger prawns, peeled and deveined
   (16 to 20 count per pound)

PRESENTATION

Seaweed salad
Thai basil, julienned
Fukujin zuke

TO MAKE MARINADE: In a bowl, whisk together lemongrass, garlic, coconut milk and fish sauce. Stir in shrimp to coat. Marinate at room temperature for 30 minutes.

TO GRILL PRAWNS: Soak 8 10-inch bamboo skewers in water for at least 30 minutes. Arrange 2 prawns on each skewer. Do not wipe off marinade, but remove pieces of lemongrass. Oil grill grate and prepare coals or preheat gas grill on high. Grill prawns over high heat for 2 to 3 minutes per side.

TO PLATE: Put 6 pickled cucumbers on 4 small plates. Top with 2 prawn skewers. Glaze with curry sauce. Top with a smidgen of seaweed salad, a sprinkling of basil and a few pieces of fukujin zuke.

MAKES 4 SERVINGS

Ahi Tartare
with wasabi tobiko

Ahi is the Hawaiian name for tuna. Only the highest-grade tuna should be used to make this dish – #1 grade, center-cut tuna, with no chain and very little or no membranes or blood. I recommend you seek out reputable specialty stores to buy the tuna. In the restaurant, we often serve the tuna with rice crackers. They come from Thailand and can be difficult to obtain, so I suggest you serve the tartare with Crispy Vegetable Chips or purchase thin, crispy crackers.

COUNTDOWN

As far ahead as desired
• Make pickled cucumbers.

Up to 4 hours ahead
• Make vegetable chips.

Just before serving
• Make tartare.

TIPS:

• It is important to keep the tuna chilled at all times.

• Always add sesame oil last. If added early to cold ingredients, it causes the mixture to become opaque.

INGREDIENTS

1 recipe Pickled Cucumbers (page 165)
1 recipe Crispy Vegetable Chips
   (page 164)

TARTARE

16 ounces center-cut sashimi grade #1
   ahi, yellowfin, bigeye, or bluefin tuna
2 shiso leaves, julienned (1 tablespoon)
¼ cup thinly sliced green onions
   with tops

¼ teaspoon shichimi togarashi (Japanese
   seven-spice)
½ teaspoon furikake (nori blend)
¼ cup soy sauce
½ teaspoon sesame oil

PRESENTATION

2 teaspoons wasabi tobiko
Furikake
Shichimi togarashi

TO PREPARE TUNA: If tuna contains any blood or membrane, cut it out. Dice tuna by first cutting it into thin slices horizontally. Julienne each slice and then cut crosswise into ¼-inch dice. You should have about 2 cups.

TO MAKE TARTARE: Put tuna into a bowl and stir in shiso leaves and green onion. Add togarashi, furikake and soy sauce. Stir very well. Last, stir in the sesame oil.

TO PLATE: Fill center of plate with a layer of cucumbers in a circle. Loosely pack tartare into an ice cream scoop or small measuring cup. Unmold onto center of cucumbers. Top with ½ teaspoon wasabi tobiko. Sprinkle furikake and togarashi lightly around plate for color. Stand chips or crackers up against tartare.

MAKES 4 SERVINGS

Grilled Alaskan Wild Ivory King Salmon

with yukon gold mashed potatoes and creamed corn

Here grilled salmon is served over fluffy mashed potatoes and creamy fresh corn. The fish is topped off with a dab of butter, flavored with either truffles or fresh herbs, and a sprinkling of truffle oil or olive oil – savory, sophisticated and mouth-watering.

TIPS:

• In the restaurant, I use wild Alaskan ivory salmon, but any fresh salmon can be substituted.

• If you want to serve truffle butter, but don't want to make it, you can purchase it from a specialty food store.

• I grill the salmon to medium-rare. Remember that it continues to cook after you remove it from the grill.

INGREDIENTS

1 recipe Creamed Corn (page 143)
1 recipe Yukon Gold Mashed Potatoes
   (page 153)
4 tablespoons unsalted butter ($\frac{1}{2}$ stick),
   softened
1 teaspoon grated fresh truffles or
   2 teaspoons mixed chopped fresh
   chervil, chives and thyme

4 salmon fillets (4 ounces each),
   1 to 1$\frac{1}{2}$ inches thick
Extra virgin olive oil

PRESENTATION
White or black truffle oil or extra virgin
   olive oil

TO MAKE BUTTER: In a small bowl, cream butter with a fork or wooden spoon. Stir in truffles or herbs until combined. Season with sea salt and pepper to taste. Butter may be used immediately or refrigerated overnight. Bring to room temperature before using.

TO GRILL SALMON: Oil grill grate and prepare coals or preheat gas grill on high. Brush salmon with olive oil and season with sea salt and pepper. Grill over high heat for 2 to 3 minutes or until brown grill marks appear on the bottom. Turn and grill other side for 2 to 4 more minutes, or until medium-rare. Cover and let rest for 5 minutes.

TO PLATE: Spoon a dollop of mashed potatoes onto 4 small plates. Spoon creamed corn over potatoes. Top with salmon. Put a spoonful of seasoned butter on salmon and drizzle with truffle or olive oil.

MAKES 4 SERVINGS

COUNTDOWN

Up to 2 days ahead
• Make truffle or herb butter.
• Make cream for creamed corn.

Up to 4 hours ahead
• Make mashed potatoes; leave covered in pan.
• Bring seasoned butter to room temperature.

45 minutes ahead
• Prepare coals.

15 minutes before serving
• Finish creamed corn.
• Grill salmon.
• Reheat potatoes.

Parma Prosciutto-Wrapped Ambrosia Melon
with beefsteak tomato sorbet

There is a reason that prosciutto and melon have been paired in Italy for decades. They go together like champagne and caviar. My only addition is to grill the prosciutto-wrapped melon for 2 minutes until the prosciutto softens. Then I serve it with a zesty tomato sorbet.

COUNTDOWN

Up to I week ahead
• Make and freeze sorbet.

30 minutes ahead
• Prepare coals.

5 minutes ahead
• Grill prosciutto.

TIP:

• Ambrosia is a hybrid muskmelon with a sweet, distinctive flavor and peach-colored flesh. If it is not available, substitute cantaloupe.

INGREDIENTS

I recipe Beefsteak Tomato Sorbet
(page 142)
I ripe ambrosia melon

8 ounces Parma prosciutto
Extra virgin olive oil
Balsamic vinegar

TO PREPARE MELON: Cut peel off of the entire melon. Cut melon in half. Scoop out seeds from one half (reserve second half for another use). Put melon flat side down on work surface. Slice lengthwise into 4 wedges. Turn over and cut each wedge into 3 slices.

TO PREPARE PROSCIUTTO: Slice prosciutto lengthwise in half. Wrap half a slice of prosciutto around each melon wedge, patching pieces as needed. Drizzle slices with olive oil and sprinkle with sea salt and pepper.

TO GRILL: Oil grill grate and prepare coals or preheat gas grill to high. Decrease heat to medium and grill prosciutto-wrapped melon for I minute on each side, or until prosciutto wilts slightly.

TO PLATE: Arrange 3 slices of wrapped melon down center of plate, fanning them out so they meet at the bottom. Drizzle with olive oil and balsamic vinegar. Put a small scoop of sorbet at the bottom of melon fan.

MAKES 4 SERVINGS

Peach and Blueberry Cobbler

For a delicious cobbler, toss ripe and juicy peaches and blueberries and blanket them with rich, buttery pastry. To enjoy a beautiful taste of summer, serve warm, crowned with the finest vanilla ice cream.

COUNTDOWN

Up to 1 day ahead
- Make pastry dough and refrigerate.

Up to 2 hours ahead
- Make and bake cobblers. Before serving, reheat at 350°F for 10 minutes or until warm.

TIPS:

- Blackberries or boysenberries may be substituted for the blueberries.
- You will need 6 (¾ cup) ramekins or soufflé dishes. Measure their capacity by pouring in ¾ cup water.
- I use tapioca flour to thicken fruit desserts because it is lighter in taste and texture than all-purpose flour or cornstarch. See Mixed Berry Crisp (page 86).
- Good, fruity cobblers are meant to bubble over the sides of the dish; these will do just that, so don't be surprised. The pastry falls a little while cooling, making a perfect indentation for the ice cream.

INGREDIENTS

SWEET PASTRY

¾ cup (1½ sticks) butter, at room temperature
⅔ cup powdered sugar
2 cups all-purpose flour
Pinch of sea salt

FILLING

8 peaches
12 ounces blueberries, rinsed and dried
¾ cup sugar
3 tablespoons tapioca flour
½ teaspoon ground cinnamon
Vanilla bean ice cream, for serving

TO MAKE PASTRY: In a mixing bowl with electric beaters, mix butter and powdered sugar until blended. Add flour and salt and mix until pastry holds together and begins to form a ball, scraping sides as needed. Remove to a work surface and shape into a flat round. Cut into 6 equal portions. Wrap in plastic wrap and refrigerate at least 1 hour or overnight.

TO PREPARE FILLING: To peel peaches, bring a pot of water to a boil. Add peaches and cook for one minute or until peel feels loose. Drain and run under cold water to stop the cooking. Using a small sharp knife, pull off peel. Slice peaches and put into a large bowl. Add blueberries, sugar, tapioca flour and cinnamon. Toss until mixed. Butter 6 ramekins and divide fruit between them.

TO ROLL PASTRY: Remove pastry from refrigerator and leave at room temperature for 10 minutes or until soft enough to roll. It must still be very cold. Roll one piece of dough between 2 sheets of parchment paper into a circle that is 1 inch wider than your ramekin. Remove top parchment paper. Place pastry round over top of filled ramekin and remove second sheet of parchment. Gently press pastry onto sides of ramekin. Remove excess pastry so it is even with the rim.

TO BAKE: Preheat oven to 350°F. Place ramekins on a foil-lined baking sheet. Bake for 40 minutes or until sides are bubbling and pastry is golden. Remove from oven and let sit at least 20 minutes before serving.

TO PLATE: Top each cobbler with a scoop of ice cream.

MAKES 6 SERVINGS

Mixed Berry Crisp

Vibrant, juicy berries – I look forward to their arrival all year long. They don't need much embellishment – a little sugar, a little flour and a crunchy streusel topping – the berry best of summer.

COUNTDOWN

Up to I day ahead
• Make streusel and refrigerate.

Up to 5 hours before serving
• Make and bake crisps. Before serving, reheat at 350°F for 10 minutes or until warm.

TIPS:

• Choose any berries you like, but I recommend limiting the variety to three. You will need about 32 ounces.

• You will need 6 (1¼ to 1½ cup) ramekins or soufflé dishes. Measure their capacity by pouring in 1¼ to 1½ cups water.

• I use tapioca flour to thicken fruit desserts because it is lighter in taste and texture than all-purpose flour or cornstarch. You may think it's not worth buying another flour just for 3 tablespoons; try it and you'll be convinced.

• After the berries are tossed with the dry ingredients, they should be baked immediately.

INGREDIENTS

STREUSEL
1 cup all-purpose flour
½ cup brown sugar, packed
¼ pound butter (1 stick), cold and cut into cubes

BERRIES
¼ to ½ cup sugar, depending on the sweetness of the berries
3 tablespoons tapioca flour

Pinch of sea salt
10 ounces blueberries, rinsed and dried (1½ cups)
10 ounces raspberries, rinsed and blotted gently (2 cups)
12 ounces strawberries, rinsed, dried, cored and thickly sliced (2 cups)
2 teaspoons fresh lemon juice
Vanilla bean ice cream, for serving

TO MAKE STREUSEL: In a medium bowl or in a food processor, mix flour and brown sugar to combine. Add butter and work with your fingers or process until mixture is the size of small peas and butter is completely coated with the flour.

TO PREPARE BERRIES: In a large bowl, stir together sugar, tapioca flour and salt. Add berries and lemon juice; toss gently to combine.

TO BAKE: Put rack in top third of oven and preheat to 350°F. Butter ramekins. Divide berries into ramekins. Sprinkle with streusel. Put ramekins on a baking sheet and bake for 30 to 35 minutes until edges are bubbling and tops are golden. Let crisp sit at least 15 minutes before serving.

TO PLATE: Top each crisp with a scoop of ice cream.

MAKES 6 SERVINGS

Fall

Fall is crush time. Winemakers only get one chance a year to make their magic happen. If things don't work out, it's tough luck until next year. If things really go bad, there may not be a next year. No pressure though...

Adding to the pressure, you can't set your own pace or schedule as you're dependent on Mother Nature, and she doesn't care what makes you happy. All you can do is sit back, smile and wait for the sugar content in the grapes to climb. Eighteen percent sugar, not on your radar. Twenty percent, okay, you have my attention. Twenty-three percent, you are almost there. Twenty-four percent, it's go time.

If you are making white wine, you dump your freshly picked grapes into the press, crank up the pressure and squeeze every last drop of juice into a tank for the next hour. If you are making red wine, you skip the press but instead remove all of the stems with a destemmer and dump them into a waiting tank. Either way yeast is added, eating away at the natural sugars of the grapes to produce alcohol. The conversion from grapes to wine has begun.

When there is no sugar left, the white wine is placed in tanks or barrels for storage. The red wine is treated to the same press experience that the white wine enjoyed before being placed in barrels as well. That's all there is. Easy. Making wine is simple. Making really good wine, however, is another matter.

With the milder weather, it's time for mild wines from the **Mild—Soft and Fruity** style. Around Thanksgiving every year, beaujolais nouveau arrives, fresh from the fall crush in France. If you have never tried this amazing fresh and fruity wine, you are in for a treat. Also delicious with Thanksgiving dinner would be a **Bold—Smooth and Silky** gruner vetliner.

-Brendan Eliason

As we transition into fall, very often we experience an Indian Summer. Taking advantage of these last warm days, keep the summer grill out and try grilling some early fall ingredients, such as radicchio or figs. Grilled figs finished with a thirty-year-old balsamic vinegar, olive oil and a little cracked pepper — Va de Vi delicious!

-Kelly Degala

Fall Recipes

Shrimp-Bottarga Risotto

Guiseppe Cagnoni, an Italian food importer, introduces me to the newest and finest Italian products. A recent surprise was bottarga, the dried roe sac of gray mullet or tuna. Mullet is preferred to tuna although it is a bit more expensive. Bottarga can be purchased at many fine Italian specialty markets. It's pricey, but can be refrigerated indefinitely and is used sparingly. Grate it like ginger (a Microplane works well) directly into the risotto and over the top of each serving. Use as much as you like; no measurement is needed.

COUNTDOWN

Up to 2 hours ahead
- Cook first step of risotto. Leave covered at room temperature.

20 minutes before serving
- Cook shrimp and finish risotto.

TIPS:

- Start the onions and garlic in an unheated pan to make sure they don't brown.
- Stir risotto gently to avoid breaking the grains.
- Sun-dried tomatoes can be pureed in a small food processor or finely chopped by hand.

INGREDIENTS
RISOTTO

3 tablespoons extra virgin olive oil
¾ cup chopped onions
1 cup Italian Arborio rice
1 tablespoon chopped roasted sun-dried tomatoes in oil, pureed
Bottarga di muggine
1 tablespoon julienned fresh basil
1 tablespoon butter, at room temperature

SHRIMP

1½ tablespoons extra virgin olive oil

1 teaspoon finely chopped garlic
6 tiger prawns, peeled and deveined (16 to 20 count per pound)
4 ounces rock shrimp
1 cup dry white wine, such as sauvignon blanc

PRESENTATION

Julienned fresh basil
Grated bottarga
Lemon oil

TO BEGIN RISOTTO: Add olive oil and onions to an unheated 12-inch skillet. Cook over medium-low heat until onions are translucent, about 4 minutes. Do not let onions brown. Add risotto and stir until all grains are coated, 1 minute. Add 1 cup of water and simmer over medium heat, stirring constantly, until absorbed. Add 1 more cup of water. Simmer, stirring, until most, but not all, of the moisture is absorbed and grains are beginning to get creamy. There should be some liquid in the bottom of the pan. Risotto can be made ahead to this point; leave covered at room temperature.

TO COOK SHRIMP: Add olive oil and garlic into an unheated 12-inch skillet. Cook over medium heat until softened and aromatic, 2 minutes. Do not brown. Add prawns and shrimp. Cook, stirring, until they begin to turn pink, 1 to 2 minutes. Season with sea salt and pepper. Add wine and 1 cup water. Bring to a slow boil and simmer for 30 seconds. With a slotted spoon, remove shrimp to a bowl and set aside.

TO FINISH RISOTTO: Stir risotto into wine broth from shrimp. Simmer over medium heat, stirring often, until almost all liquid is absorbed and grains are almost tender. Stir in shrimp and tomato puree. Season generously with sea salt and pepper. Risotto is done when the rice is creamy and the grains are soft, but there is slight pressure in the center when bitten into. Grate enough bottarga over the top to coat it. Stir it in with the basil and butter.

TO PLATE: Spoon risotto onto 6 small plates. Place a prawn on top of each. Sprinkle with basil. Grate bottarga over and drizzle with lemon oil.

MAKES 6 SERVINGS

Hoisin-Glazed Lamb Chops
with wasabi mashed potatoes

When the weather turns cold, I often roast chops in the oven instead of grilling them. If you prefer to grill them, follow the technique for Grilled Rosemary and Garlic-Crusted Lamb Chops (page 56). After marinating the chops in a robust rosemary and garlic marinade, I give them an Asian twist by thickly coating the meat with a zesty barbecue sauce made with hoisin, oyster and plum sauces. A spoonful of wasabi stirred into mashed potatoes turns them into the perfect partner.

TIPS:

- To quickly remove rosemary stems from leaves, squeeze the top of the stem and run your fingers down the stem to separate the leaves as you go.
- Ask the butcher to French the bones, which means to cut the bottom part of the meat so the bone is exposed.
- If your skillet doesn't have an ovenproof handle, wrap it in a double thickness of foil.

INGREDIENTS

1½ recipe Hoisin Barbecue Sauce (page 156)
1 recipe Wasabi Mashed Potatoes (page 153)

ROSEMARY GARLIC MARINADE
1 cup extra virgin olive oil
1 cup fresh rosemary, stemmed
1 shallot, peeled
6 cloves garlic, peeled

2 dried or fresh bay leaves
1 tablespoon juniper berries
1 tablespoon black peppercorns

One 8-rib rack of lamb (1¼ to 1½ pounds)
1 tablespoon olive oil
PRESENTATION
Watercress
Toasted sesame seeds

TO MAKE MARINADE: In a blender or food processor, process all marinade ingredients until blended. Use immediately or refrigerate overnight. Bring to room temperature and whisk well before using. Makes about 1½ cups.

TO PREPARE AND MARINATE LAMB: Cut between bones to make 4 servings of 2 chops each. Score fat side of chops by cutting thin diagonal cuts on the surface. Turn ribs over and make shallow cuts on the meat between the bones. Place chops in a plastic zipper bag. Pour marinade over, tossing to coat. Refrigerate overnight, turning occasionally. Bring to room temperature in marinade at least one hour before cooking.

TO COOK LAMB: Preheat oven to 375°F. In a large skillet with an ovenproof handle, heat olive oil over medium-high heat until very hot and almost smoking. Remove lamb from marinade (do not wipe off marinade) and season with sea salt and pepper. Put in skillet, meat side down. Sear until well-browned, 3 to 4 minutes. Turn chops bone side down. Transfer skillet to oven. Roast chops for 12 to 15 minutes for medium-rare. Meat should register 125°F on a meat thermometer. Tent with foil and let rest for 10 minutes for the juices to settle. Carve into individual chops. Brush chops generously with barbecue sauce.

COUNTDOWN

Up to 2 weeks ahead
- Make barbecue sauce.

1 day ahead
- Make marinade and marinate lamb.

90 minutes ahead
- Bring lamb to room temperature in marinade.
- Bring barbecue sauce to room temperature.
- Make mashed potatoes; leave covered in pan.
- Prepare coals.

30 minutes ahead
- Cook lamb.

Before serving
- Reheat mashed potatoes.

TO PLATE: Spoon mashed potatoes onto the back half of 4 small plates. Arrange 2 chops standing in an 'X' in front of potatoes. Arrange a generous bunch of watercress on the side. Sprinkle toasted sesame seeds over meat and potatoes.

MAKES 4 SERVINGS

Pan-Fried Kurobuta Pork Chops

with exotic mushroom ragout and yukon gold mashed potatoes

Kurobuta pork comes from black pigs and is considered to be of superior quality. There are several components to this recipe, but both the mushroom ragout and caramelized onions serve a dual purpose. They are served alongside the pork to enhance it and also added to the gravy to enrich it. My daughter, Ariel, who is mostly vegetarian, makes an exception for this dish. Try it and you'll see why.

TIPS:

- I always marinate pork in milk because I believe it tenderizes the meat.
- If your skillet does not have an ovenproof handle, cover the handle with a double thickness of aluminum foil.

INGREDIENTS

1 recipe Yukon Gold Mashed Potatoes
   (page 153)
2 recipes Exotic Mushroom Ragout
   (page 144), divided

PORK MARINADE
6 garlic cloves, coarsely chopped
1 cup milk
4 pork loin center-cut chops, cut
   ½ inch thick

CARAMELIZED ONIONS
2 tablespoons olive oil
2 medium yellow onions, peeled, cut in
   half and thinly sliced

MUSHROOM ONION GRAVY
3 tablespoons butter
2 tablespoons chopped garlic
¼ cup dry white wine, such as
   sauvignon blanc
½ cup chicken broth
½ cup cream

PORK CHOPS
½ cup all-purpose flour
2 eggs
3 tablespoons olive oil

COUNTDOWN

Up to 1 day ahead
- Make caramelized onions and refrigerate.
- Make mushroom ragout and refrigerate.

4 to 6 hours ahead
- Marinate pork.

Up to 4 hours ahead
- Make mashed potatoes; keep covered in pan.

Up to 2 hours ahead
- Make mushroom onion gravy. If it gets too thick, thin with additional cream.

20 minutes before serving
- Dredge chops; sauté and bake.

Just before serving
- Reheat mushroom ragout.
- Reheat onions on top of stove or in microwave.
- Reheat mashed potatoes.
- Reheat gravy.

TO MARINATE PORK: Put chops close together in a casserole dish. Sprinkle with garlic and pour milk over. Lift chops to allow milk to flow underneath. Refrigerate covered 4 to 6 hours, turning once.

TO MAKE CARAMELIZED ONIONS: In a 12-inch skillet over medium-high heat, heat olive oil until hot. Add onion slices and cook, stirring constantly, until nutty brown in color, 6 to 8 minutes. Transfer to a bowl. Onions may be used immediately or refrigerated. Reheat before using.

TO MAKE GRAVY: Melt butter in a medium saucepan over medium heat. Add garlic and sauté for 1 minute until aromatic. Stir in wine. Decrease heat to medium-low and cook until wine is reduced by one-half, 2 to 3 minutes. Stir in chicken broth and cream. Simmer until reduced by about one-third, 5 to 6 minutes. Stir in half the caramelized onions. Remove from heat. With an immersion blender, puree gravy in the pan, or transfer to a blender, blend until pureed and return to saucepan. Stir in half the mushroom ragout. Season with sea salt and pepper to taste. If made ahead, keep covered in a warm place. Reheat before use.

TO COOK PORK: Preheat oven to 350°F. Put flour into a shallow dish. Whisk eggs in another shallow dish until blended. Remove chops from milk; do not dry. Season both sides with sea salt and pepper. Dredge chops in flour to coat both sides and then dip into eggs. Heat oil in a large skillet with an ovenproof handle over medium heat until hot. Put chops into skillet and cook over medium heat until golden on the bottom, 2 to 3 minutes. Turn and brown other side, 2 to 3 more minutes. If chops brown too fast or slow, decrease or increase the heat. Transfer skillet to oven and bake chops for 6 to 8 minutes or until medium.

TO PLATE: Reheat remaining mushroom ragout and onions. Spoon mushroom ragout into the center of 4 plates. Top with a pork chop. Divide onions over chops. Spoon a dollop of mashed potatoes on the side. Spoon gravy over all.

MAKES 4 SERVINGS

Pan-Fried Dungeness Crab Cakes
with aioli and citrus butter sauce

Great crab cakes should be golden and crispy on the outside and loaded with crab meat and spices within. They should have just enough mayonnaise and bread crumbs to hold them together. When you taste these crab cakes, I know you'll agree – they are great.

COUNTDOWN

Up to 2 days ahead
• Make aioli and refrigerate.

1 day ahead
• Make crab cakes, cover and refrigerate.

2 hours ahead
• Make butter sauce up to the point of adding butter.

20 minutes before serving
• Bread, pan-fry and bake crab cakes.
• Finish butter sauce.

TIPS:

• To help the crab mixture hold together, refrigerate the cakes before cooking them.

• I prefer using panko (Japanese breadcrumbs) because they make a beautiful, crispy crust when used in frying.

• For an even coating, process panko crumbs in the processor until they are ground.

• If you make smaller cakes, they make terrific hors d'oeuvres.

INGREDIENTS

1 recipe Aioli (page 157)
1 recipe Citrus Butter Sauce (page 155)
CRAB CAKES
2½ cups panko
¼ cup loosely packed Italian
    parsley leaves
1 pound Dungeness crab meat
1 teaspoon finely chopped garlic
½ cup diced red bell pepper
¼ cup diced red onion

1 tablespoon Dijon mustard
½ teaspoon hot red pepper sauce
¼ teaspoon sea salt
½ teaspoon freshly ground pepper
¾ cup mayonnaise
4 tablespoons vegetable oil, divided
PRESENTATION
1 avocado, sliced
Lemon oil

TO MAKE CRAB CAKES: Process panko in food processor until evenly ground. Add parsley and process until finely chopped. Reserve ½ cup and transfer remainder to a pie dish. In a large bowl, gently toss crab meat, garlic, bell pepper, onion, mustard, pepper sauce, salt, and pepper. Gently stir in reserved ½ cup panko and mayonnaise until combined. Line a baking sheet with foil. Fill a ½ cup measure with crab mixture. Drop onto baking sheet. Repeat, making 8 mounds. With hands, flatten into patties about 2½ inches round by ½ inch thick. Cover and refrigerate for at least one hour or overnight.

TO COAT: Press both sides and edges of crab cakes into remaining panko in pie dish, pressing lightly to adhere. Return to baking sheet. Sprinkle any remaining crumbs over the top and press in lightly.

TO COOK: Pre-heat oven to 450°F. In a large skillet over high heat, heat 2 tablespoons oil until almost smoking. Test the oil by adding a few bread crumbs to it; the oil should bubble around it. Add half the crab cakes and cook until bottoms are golden brown, 45 to 60 seconds. Turn and brown other side, 60 seconds. Return cakes to baking sheet. Repeat with remaining cakes, adding more oil as needed. Place baking sheet in oven and cook for 2 minutes. Turn and cook 2 more minutes.

TO PLATE: Place 2 crab cakes on a small plate. Spoon an arc of citrus butter around half the plate. Top each cake with a dollop of aioli and a slice of avocado. Spoon 2 dots of aioli on avocado. Sprinkle lemon oil over crab cakes.

MAKES 4 SERVINGS: 2 CRAB CAKES EACH

Lacquered Quail
with ono garlic fried rice and fried spinach

When you're looking for something new and different to make for a dinner party, try this recipe. It is very easy to make and judging by its popularity in the restaurant, you'll be happy you did. A sweetly-glazed bird with charred and crackly skin and juicy meat is a special taste treat.

TIP:

- Many supermarkets sell fresh, semi-boned quail. It is a good idea to order ahead.

INGREDIENTS

1 recipe Crispy Fried Spinach (page 163)
1 recipe Green Onion Curls (page 164)
1 recipe Ono Garlic Fried Rice
   (page 150)

KALBI MARINADE

1 cup soy sauce
¼ cup vegetable oil
1 teaspoon sesame oil
1 tablespoon finely chopped ginger

1 tablespoon honey
1 cup packed golden brown sugar
2 tablespoons toasted sesame seeds
1 green onion with top, thinly sliced
1 teaspoon freshly ground pepper
1 teaspoon crushed red chili flakes

4 quails, semi-boned, rinsed and dried
1 tablespoon cornstarch

COUNTDOWN

Up to 2 weeks ahead
- Make kalbi marinade and refrigerate.

Up to 1 day ahead
- Make green onion curls .

3 hours ahead
- Bring marinade to room temperature.

2 hours ahead
- Marinate quail.
- Make fried spinach.

45 minutes ahead
- Prepare coals.

20 minutes ahead
- Prepare rice.
- Make glaze.

15 minutes ahead
- Grill quail.

TO MAKE MARINADE: Measure all ingredients into a deep bowl and whisk until blended. Use immediately or refrigerate. Bring to room temperature and whisk before using. Makes 2 cups.

TO PREPARE AND MARINATE QUAIL: Cut off quail's wing tip and second joint. Place quail into a plastic zipper bag. Pour in 1 cup marinade and toss to coat. Marinate at room temperature for 1 to 2 hours, turning occasionally.

TO MAKE GLAZE: Pour ½ cup reserved marinade into a small saucepan. Bring to a simmer. Dissolve cornstarch in 1 tablespoon water. Stir dissolved cornstarch into marinade. Bring to a boil, stirring, and remove from heat. Glaze should be thickened slightly.

TO GRILL: Oil grill grate and prepare coals or preheat gas grill to high. Remove quail from marinade. Discard marinade. Put remaining ½ cup reserved marinade in a medium bowl. Grill quail breast side up over medium heat, basting with reserved marinade and moving quail around, until nicely charred, about 5 minutes. Turn and grill breast side down, basting and turning until charred and cooked through, 5 more minutes. Remove to a cutting board and cut in half lengthwise.

TO PLATE: Spoon rice in center of 4 small plates. Put one half quail over rice and the second half over the first in the opposite direction. Reheat glaze if necessary, and spoon over quail; garnish each side with fried spinach. Top quail with green onion curls.

MAKES 4 SERVINGS

Seared Hawaiian Bigeye Tuna

with sake-wasabi butter sauce on potato croquette

This delicious contrast of tastes and textures features a creamy wasabi-tinged sauce topped with a crispy potato croquette and rare slices of juicy tuna capped with pickled ginger, ponzu and a sprinkling of Asian flavorings.

TIPS:

*   You will end up with two extra potato croquettes. Enjoy them for another meal or prepare the tuna for six; you will need to purchase 6 to 8 more ounces of tuna. The sauce will be adequate for 6 servings.
*   Instead of searing the tuna, it may be grilled over high heat for 30 to 60 seconds per side.

INGREDIENTS

1 recipe Potato Croquettes (page 151)
1 recipe Sake-Wasabi Butter Sauce
     (page 155)
1 recipe Tempura Enoki (page 166)

TUNA

12 to 16 ounces sashimi grade #1 bigeye
     tuna, cut into four 1-inch-thick steaks
1 tablespoon olive oil
Freshly ground pepper

PRESENTATION

Seaweed salad
Pickled ginger
Ponzu
Shichimi togarashi
     (Japanese seven-spice)
Furikake (nori flakes)
Red tobiko
Wasabi tobiko

TO COOK TUNA: Heat a large skillet over high heat until very hot. Brush both sides of tuna with oil and sprinkle with pepper. Place in pan; it should sizzle and smoke. Sear for 45 to 60 seconds until bottom is golden. Turn and sear for 30 to 45 seconds. Remove from heat. Slice ¼ inch thick.

TO PLATE: Spoon enough butter sauce to cover bottom of 4 small plates. Place a potato croquette in the center of the sauce. Top croquette with slices of tuna and enoki mushrooms . Place a few mushrooms on top of tuna. Spoon a dollop of seaweed salad and 2 slices of pickled ginger on top. Drizzle with ponzu and sprinkle with togarashi and furikake. Top with a spoonful of red tobiko and wasabi tobiko.

MAKES 4 SERVINGS

COUNTDOWN

Up to 1 day ahead
*   Make croquettes and refrigerate.

Up to 2 hours ahead
*   Make butter sauce up to the point of adding butter. Cover and keep at room temperature.

Just before serving
*   Finish sauce.
*   Make mushrooms.
*   Cook tuna.

Moi à la Piccata

Moi is the Hawaiian name for Pacific threadfin. It is a white and flaky fish with mild ocean flavor. In ancient history, moi were so revered that only Hawaiian royalty were allowed to eat them. When you taste the tender white fish fillets swimming in a buttery lemon sauce, dotted with whole caperberries and preserved lemon slices, I'm sure you'll agree that this dish is fit for a king.

COUNTDOWN

Up to 4 hours ahead
• Cook potatoes and onions.

10 minutes before serving
• Sauté fish.

5 minutes before serving
• Reheat potatoes and onions.
• Make sauce.

TIPS:

• Good substitutes for moi are opakapaka, striped bass and Tai snapper.

• You can purchase Moroccan preserved lemon slices at specialty food stores and Middle Eastern markets. Fresh lemon slices may be substituted, if desired.

• To keep fillets from curling in the pan, start them meat side down.

• If you double the recipe, sauté the fish in 2 batches to avoid overcrowding the pan.

INGREDIENTS

2 cipollini onions, ends trimmed and peeled

2 fingerling potatoes, scrubbed and dried

1½ teaspoons plus 2 tablespoons extra virgin olive oil

2 moi fillets (4 to 6 ounces each), with skin

¼ cup all-purpose flour

4 whole caperberries with stems

8 preserved half-lemon slices

½ cup dry white wine, such as sauvignon blanc

2 tablespoons fresh lemon juice

2 tablespoons whole Italian parsley leaves

¼ cup (½ stick) unsalted butter, at room temperature

TO BAKE ONIONS AND POTATOES: Preheat oven to 400°F. Put onions and potatoes into a shallow baking pan. Drizzle with 1½ teaspoons oil; toss to coat. Sprinkle with sea salt. Cover with foil. Bake for 10 to 15 minutes or until onions give a little when centers are pierced with a skewer. Remove onions. Cover potatoes and bake 20 more minutes or until almost tender. Remove foil and continue to bake uncovered for 10 minutes or until tender. Cut potatoes in half lengthwise.

TO COOK FISH: Put flour in pie pan. Season fish with sea salt and pepper. Dip both sides in flour, patting off the excess. In a 12-inch nonstick skillet over medium-high heat, heat 2 tablespoons oil until hot, but not smoking. Add fish, meat side down; it should sizzle. Cook until undersides are golden, about 4 minutes. Turn and cook until skin is golden, about 2 minutes. Remove fish to plate and cover with foil or put in warming drawer.

TO MAKE SAUCE: Add potatoes, skin side down, and onions to pan. Sauté over medium-low heat until hot, about 2 minutes. Add caperberries, preserved lemons, wine and lemon juice. Bring to a boil and simmer 2 minutes. Turn heat to lowest setting. Add parsley and butter, whisking butter until it melts and sauce is smooth and creamy. Do not overcook or sauce will break and thin down. Season with sea salt and pepper.

TO PLATE: Put 2 potato halves, 2 onions and 2 caperberries removed from sauce on 2 small plates. Top with fish, skin side up. Drizzle with sauce. Spoon remaining sauce around bottom of plates.

MAKES 2 SERVINGS

Grilled Skirt Steak
with creamed corn, mashed potatoes and beef jus with mushroom ragout

I make this recipe with hangar steak in the restaurant. However, I learned that hangar steak is not readily available in meat markets so I decided to test it with skirt steak. I must admit, I was favorably impressed with the outcome. If possible, ask the butcher for skirt steaks that are ½ inch thick. They make an extremely good substitute for hangar steak.

TIP:
- The ingredients in the beef jus can be coarsely chopped because they will be strained out before using. That is the reason you can add the thyme leaves attached to the woody stems.

INGREDIENTS
1 cup Exotic Mushroom Ragout (page 144)
1 recipe Creamed Corn (page 143)
1 recipe Yukon Gold Mashed Potatoes (page 153)
1 recipe Crispy Fried Shallots (page 162)

GARLIC AND THYME MARINADE
1 cup extra virgin olive oil
1 shallot, peeled and quartered
6 cloves garlic, peeled
½ cup thyme leaves (¾ ounces on stems)
1 tablespoon black peppercorns
1 cup parsley leaves
1 dried or fresh bay leaf

1 pound skirt steaks, preferably ½ inch thick, cut into 4 pieces

BEEF JUS
1 tablespoon butter
4 garlic cloves, peeled and chopped
2 shallots, peeled and chopped
4 stems fresh thyme, coarsely chopped
¾ cup dry red wine, such as cabernet sauvignon
1 tablespoon black peppercorns
⅓ cup beef demi-glace dissolved in ½ cup water

PRESENTATION
Porcini oil

COUNTDOWN

1 day ahead
- Marinate meat and refrigerate.

Up to 1 day ahead
- Make beef jus and refrigerate.
- Make mushroom ragout and refrigerate.
- Make cream for creamed corn and refrigerate.

4 hours ahead
- Marinate meat at room temperature.

Up to 4 hours ahead
- Make mashed potatoes; leave covered in pan.
- Make fried shallots.

1 hour ahead
- Prepare coals.

20 minutes before serving
- Finish creamed corn.
- Heat jus and stir in the mushrooms.
- Heat mashed potatoes.
- Grill steaks.

TO MAKE MARINADE: In a blender, blend all ingredients until pureed. Use immediately or refrigerate up to 2 days. Bring to room temperature and whisk well before using. Makes 1 cup.

TO MARINATE STEAKS: Put steaks into a large plastic zipper bag. Add marinade and toss to coat. Refrigerate overnight, turning occasionally. Remove to room temperature about 4 hours before grilling.

TO MAKE BEEF JUS: In a small saucepan over medium heat, melt butter. Stir in garlic and shallots and sauté until translucent and aromatic, about 2 minutes. Add remaining ingredients, except mushroom ragout. Simmer over medium-low heat until it is a rich brown color and reduced to ¾ cup, about 40 minutes. Strain and return to saucepan. Before serving, reheat and stir in mushroom ragout. Season with sea salt and pepper to taste.

TO GRILL STEAKS: Oil grill grate and prepare coals or preheat a gas grill on high heat. Remove steaks from marinade (do not remove excess marinade from meat) and season with sea salt and pepper. Grill steaks until charred, about 2 minutes. If flames flare up, douse them with water. Turn and char other side,

2 minutes. Grill, turning occasionally, until medium-rare, 125°F on a meat thermometer, 5 to 6 minutes total. Remove from heat to a cutting board. Tent with foil and let sit for 10 minutes for the juices to settle. Carve across the grain into thin slices.

TO PLATE: Spoon mashed potatoes onto one side of small plate and creamed corn onto the other side. Top with strips of steak, laying two in one direction, two across and two more on top in the same direction as the first. Spoon beef jus over and drizzle with porcini oil. Garnish the top with fried shallots.

MAKES 4 SERVINGS

John Dory
with truffle mashed potatoes and chervil butter sauce

In the restaurant I make this with either John Dory or ocean trout, depending upon which is available. I can't think of any mild white fish fillets that wouldn't benefit from this velvety chervil butter sauce, topped with black truffle oil.

INGREDIENTS

½ recipe Truffle Mashed Potatoes
   (page 153)
1 recipe Chervil Butter Sauce
   (page 155)
4 John Dory fillets
   (6 ounces each), skinned

½ cup all-purpose flour
3 tablespoons extra virgin olive oil

PRESENTATION

4 sprigs fresh chervil
Black truffle oil

COUNTDOWN

Up to 4 hours ahead
• Make mashed potatoes; leave covered in pan.

Up to 2 hours ahead
• Make chervil butter sauce up to point of adding butter. Keep at room temperature.

20 minutes before serving
• Prepare and pan-fry fish.
• Finish butter sauce while fish is in oven.
• Reheat mashed potatoes.

TO COOK FISH: Preheat oven to 375°F. Cut each fillet lengthwise down the center making 8 strips of fish. Season one side with sea salt and pepper. Place flour in a shallow bowl. Dredge fish in flour. In a 12-inch skillet, preferably nonstick, over medium-high heat, heat oil until hot. Add half the fish and pan fry until golden on the bottom, 2 minutes. Turn and brown other side, 1 to 2 minutes. Remove to baking sheet. Repeat with remaining fish. Put fish in oven and bake for 5 to 6 minutes or until cooked through.

TO PLATE: Spoon mashed potatoes into the bottom of 4 shallow soup bowls. Place 1 slice of fish on top of potatoes. Place second slice across first in opposite direction. Spoon 1 tablespoon butter sauce over fish. Garnish with a sprig of chervil. Drizzle with truffle oil and sprinkle with freshly ground pepper to taste.

MAKES 4 SERVINGS

Seared John Dory
with Double Mash,
Citrus Butter & Herb Oil

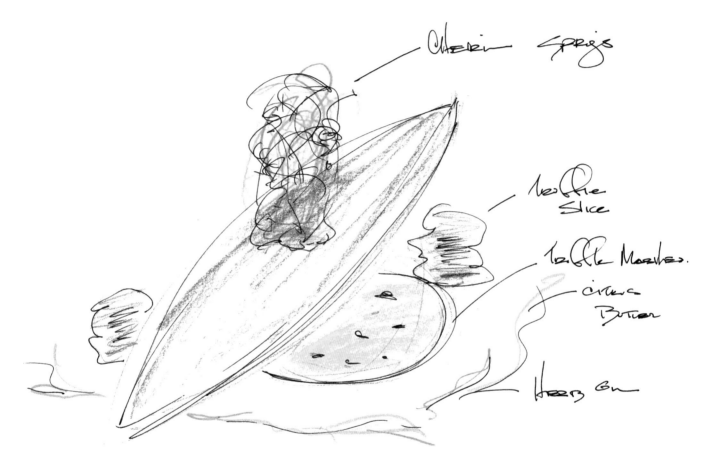

Chervil Sprigs

Double Slice

Double Mashes.

Citrus Butter

Herb Oil

Long Plate

Grilled Radicchio and Porcini Mushroom Salad

with smoked idiazabal and fig balsamic vinaigrette

I often use radicchio leaves as cups to fill with ratatouille and other brown-hued dishes that need color for presentation. I was just using the cups and was never able to use up the whole head. I created this salad as a way of using the leftover leaves, but it became so popular that I was purchasing more radicchio just to make this salad. A simple dressing of fig balsamic vinegar and orange olive oil sweetens the astringent taste of the lettuce.

TIPS:

- Idiazabal, a Basque smoked raw sheep cheese, is grated over the top.
- Manchego may be substituted for the Idiazabal.
- Grilling radicchio helps minimize its bitterness.

INGREDIENTS

FIG BALSAMIC VINAIGRETTE
¼ cup extra virgin olive oil
¼ cup orange oil
¼ cup fig balsamic vinegar

SALAD
4 ounces porcini mushrooms

1 head radicchio (about 12 ounces), quartered through the core
Olive oil
1 bunch frisée (curly greens), leaves separated and cleaned

PRESENTATION
Grated Idiazabal cheese

TO MAKE DRESSING: In a small bowl, whisk oils and vinegar until emulsified. Keep at room temperature. Whisk well before using.

TO GRILL RADICCHIO AND MUSHROOMS: Wipe porcini with a damp cloth and slice into 3 or 4 thick slices. Put porcini and radicchio into a bowl. Add olive oil and toss to coat. Season with sea salt and pepper and toss again. Oil grill rack and prepare coals or preheat gas grill on high. Grill loose radicchio leaves, porcini slices and radicchio quarters over high heat, turning often, until browned. Radicchio leaves take 1 to 2 minutes, porcini slices 4 to 5 minutes and radicchio quarters, 5 to 6 minutes. Radicchio quarters are done when the leaves fan out and begin to separate. Cool and cut out core from radicchio quarters and discard. Slice porcini into strips. Place mushrooms and radicchio in a bowl and keep at room temperature.

TO PLATE: Add frisée to radicchio and mushrooms and toss with enough dressing to coat. Divide salad between 4 small plates. Grate cheese over top. Grind pepper over all.

MAKES 4 SERVINGS

COUNTDOWN

Up to 8 hours ahead
- Make vinaigrette; keep at room temperature.

Up to 4½ hours ahead
- Prepare coals.

Up to 4 hours ahead
- Grill radicchio and porcini mushrooms; keep at room temperature.

Just before serving
- Whisk dressing and toss salad.

Vanilla Bean Leche Flan

My customers tell me that this is the best flan they've ever tasted because it is so rich, velvety and creamy. It bakes for a long time, almost 3 hours, in a very slow oven. Sometimes I consider cooking it faster, but "if it's not broken, don't fix it."

COUNTDOWN

1 day before serving
- Flan should be made at least one day before serving. It may be refrigerated for up to 2 days.

INGREDIENTS

CARAMEL
1 cup sugar
¼ cup water

CUSTARD
2 cups heavy whipping cream
One 3-inch vanilla bean
6 egg yolks

2 whole eggs
1 can (14 ounces) sweetened
    condensed milk

PRESENTATION
Powdered sugar
Edible flowers (optional)

Preheat oven to 300°F. You will need a loaf pan (preferably glass) that is 9 by 5 by 3 inches. Choose a 3- to 4-inch-deep baking pan that the loaf pan fits in. It will be used as a water bath. Set aside.

TO MAKE CARAMEL: In a small saucepan, preferably not dark so you can see the color of the sugar, bring sugar and water to a boil over medium heat, stirring once if needed to help dissolve sugar. Boil, without stirring, until sugar turns mahogany, about 5 minutes. When it begins turning brown, it is alright to stir again. Watch carefully, as it goes from mahogany to burnt very quickly. Pour caramel into loaf pan. Immediately pick up loaf pan with potholders and swirl to coat bottom and as far up the sides as possible with caramel. It will be thicker on the bottom. Set aside to cool and harden.

TO INFUSE CREAM: Pour cream into a medium saucepan. Slit vanilla bean down the center and with the tip of a sharp knife scrape seeds into cream. Add vanilla bean. Heat over medium-high heat until bubbles appear around the edge. Whisk to disperse vanilla. Remove from heat and cool to room temperature.

TO MAKE CUSTARD: In a large bowl, whisk egg yolks and eggs until blended. Add cooled cream and condensed milk and whisk until combined. Pour through a strainer into loaf pan. Cover with foil.

TO BAKE: Put loaf pan into larger pan and put in oven. Add enough boiling water to larger pan to come 1 inch up sides of loaf pan. Bake for 2 hours and 45 to 50 minutes or until center jiggles slightly when shaken. It will firm up as it cools. Cool to room temperature. Refrigerate, covered, until thoroughly chilled, preferably overnight.

TO UNMOLD: Go around edge of custard with the tip of a small knife. Invert onto a large platter that has a small rim or lip to hold the caramel. The caramel will coat the flan and puddle on the plate. Refrigerate until serving. To remove hardened caramel in bottom of loaf pan, pour in an inch of water and microwave until bubbling. Rinse in hot water.

TO PLATE: Slice flan and spoon some of the caramel over each slice. Sprinkle plate with powdered sugar. If desired, garnish with edible flowers.

MAKES 10 TO 12 SERVINGS

Winter

After the frantic excitement of the crush, winter can be downright boring. In the winery, the wine is happily sleeping away. A little lab work and a minor amount of maintenance is all that is necessary. There is, however, at least one major job left in the field to do, which is to give the vines their yearly haircut.

Once the grapes have been picked, each vine is left as an empty shell consisting of a central trunk, dozens of canes extending from it, and hundreds of buds evenly spaced along these canes. The vine only needs thirty to forty buds to produce a crop next year. Everything else goes.

Armed with waterproof boots, warm jackets and sharp shears, a small army of vineyard workers descends into the vines to carefully snip and contour each vine. What they leave behind is a well-manicured vine that is ready to produce next year's crop and a small pile of clippings ready to be composted into the earth. Once this is complete, everyone takes a deep breath and relaxes until spring when it is time to start over again.

With hearty food, winter is the time to enjoy hearty wines, like the **Voluptuous – Full and Oaky** white wines such as rich and oaky chardonnay, or a **Burly – Dense and Intense** red wine like a Napa Valley cabernet sauvignon.

-Brendan Eliason

The pace of life decelerates and so do our cooking techniques as we embrace braising, roasting and slow cooking. Braised short ribs that melt in your mouth are a winter staple as is roast duck breast. Lentils and beets round out this hearty fare.

-Kelly Degala

Winter Recipes

Rock Shrimp and Avocado Lumpia

with wasabi-orange cream

These are so popular that preparing them has become the sole responsibility of one of the kitchen staff. Everyone seems to love this combination of shrimp and avocado encased in a crisp and flaky lumpia wrap. These may look like Chinese egg rolls, but the unique, creamy filling defies that comparison.

TIP:

• Lumpia wraps are very much like filo sheets; fresh are easier to work with than frozen. After they are frozen, they may be difficult to separate. Save any torn sheets; they work well as a second wrap to use over those that tear while rolling. To ensure wraps don't dry out, cover them with a moist towel while working.

COUNTDOWN

Up to 1 week ahead
• Make wasabi-orange cream and refrigerate.

Up to 4 hours ahead
• Prepare lumpia and place on a baking sheet. Cover with a damp towel and refrigerate.

Up to 2 hours ahead
• Bring wasabi-orange cream to room temperature.

Just before serving
• Fry lumpia.

INGREDIENTS

1 recipe Wasabi-Orange Cream (page 161)

FILLING

2 tablespoons olive oil
1 pound rock shrimp
½ cup finely chopped red bell pepper
¼ cup finely chopped red onion
½ teaspoon hot red pepper sauce
1 tablespoon Dijon mustard
½ teaspoon sea salt
1 teaspoon finely chopped garlic
⅔ cup mayonnaise

12 lumpia wrappers, 6 or 8 inches square or round
2 avocados, peeled and thinly sliced
1 egg mixed with 1 teaspoon water, for wash
Cornstarch
Vegetable oil for frying

PRESENTATION

Seaweed salad
Ponzu
Pickled ginger
Furikake (nori blend)

TO MAKE FILLING: In a 12-inch skillet over medium-high heat, heat oil until hot. Add shrimp and sauté until cooked through, 2 to 3 minutes. Season with sea salt and pepper. Drain in colander in sink until cool. Coarsely chop into large pieces. In a large bowl, stir together bell pepper, onion and shrimp. Stir in pepper sauce, mustard, ½ teaspoon sea salt and pepper to taste. Add garlic and mayonnaise; stir to combine.

TO WRAP: Carefully separate 12 lumpia wrappers and lay them out on a work surface. If using square wrappers, place them in a diamond shape with a pointed edge toward you. Place 2 thin slices of avocado in the center. Top each with ¼ cup shrimp filling. Brush egg wash over top half of wrapper. Fold bottom edge over filling; pull it towards you to tighten the filling into a log shape. Fold sides over filling and roll into a tight log. If the lumpia tears, roll in a second wrapper. (Don't add a third wrapper; it will be too thick.) Pour some cornstarch into a pie dish. Roll each lumpia lightly in cornstarch and place on a baking sheet.

TO FRY: Fill a deep fryer or Dutch oven with several inches of oil. Heat to 360°F. Lumpia will need to be cooked in batches. Carefully add lumpia to oil without crowding; leave enough room to turn them. Fry, turning with tongs until golden brown on all sides, 3 to 4 minutes. Remove to a baking sheet lined with paper towels.

TO PLATE: Lightly sprinkle center of plate with seaweed salad. Using a serrated knife cut ends off lumpia and cut lumpia into quarters. Stand 8 pieces on a plate, filling side up. Place ends next to rolls. Sprinkle tops lightly with ponzu. Add 2 slices of pickled ginger on top. Spoon a dollop of orange cream next to rolls. Sprinkle with furikake.

MAKES 6 SERVINGS

Endive and Frisée Salad
with gala apples, marcona almonds and roquefort

Endive has a slightly bitter taste, which I counter with sweet apple and tangy Roquefort cheese. For a fresh and attractive presentation, I serve the endive leaves whole. Toasted Spanish Marcona almonds top the salad with a salty crunch.

TIP:

• In the restaurant I use French Carles Roquefort, but any raw sheep's milk Roquefort would make a good substitute.

COUNTDOWN

Up to 2 weeks ahead
• Make Roquefort dressing and refrigerate.

Up to 4 hours ahead
• Rinse and dry frisée. Wrap frisée in damp paper towels and put into a plastic bag; refrigerate.

Just before serving
• Assemble and toss salad.

INGREDIENTS
ROQUEFORT DRESSING

1 cup crumbled raw sheep's milk
   Roquefort cheese (about 4 ounces)
¾ cup buttermilk
1½ tablespoons Banyul or
   champagne vinegar
Freshly ground pepper

SALAD

1 head frisée (6 ounces)
1 head red Belgian endive (3 ounces),
   rinsed and dried
1 head yellow Belgian endive
   (3 ounces), rinsed and dried
1 gala apple, peeled and thinly sliced
½ cup crumbled Roquefort cheese
½ cup Marcona Spanish almonds

PRESENTATION

Coarsely ground pepper
Marcona almonds
Crumbled Roquefort cheese

TO MAKE DRESSING: Blend cheese, buttermilk and vinegar in blender until creamy. Season with pepper. Refrigerate until using. Makes 1¼ cups.

TO MAKE SALAD: Trim the core of the frisée. Rinse leaves several times to ensure all grit is removed. Dry well. Tear frilly tops of leaves into bite-size pieces and put into a salad bowl. Remove outer leaves of Belgian endive and discard. Cut a thin slice off the bottom and separate leaves, cutting the bottom as needed in order to remove the leaves. Add to frisée. Add apple, Roquefort crumbles and almonds. Toss with as much dressing as desired.

TO PLATE: Divide salad between 4 small plates. Season with coarsely ground pepper. Top with a few almonds and a sprinkling of cheese.

MAKES 4 SERVINGS

umbrian Lentils

with braised sardinian-style sausage

On a chilly winter's eve, this hearty dish of earthy lentils and Italian sausage simmered in beef broth and spices will warm your body and soul.

TIPS:

- Although many packages say to soak lentils, in this recipe no soaking is needed.

- The recipe can be doubled and cooked in a Dutch oven instead of a skillet.

- This dish can be made vegetarian by omitting the sausages and substituting vegetable broth for the beef broth.

INGREDIENTS

1 recipe Crispy Fried Sage Leaves (page 162)

1¼ cups Umbrian lentils, such as Lenticchie brand (about 8 ounces)

4 cloves garlic, peeled

2 sprigs fresh thyme

2 tablespoons extra virgin olive oil

⅓ cup chopped onions

1 tablespoon finely chopped garlic

4 mild Italian sausages (about 1 pound)

1½ cups beef broth

1 can (15 ounces) whole tomatoes in juice

¾ teaspoon sea salt

1 tablespoon chopped Italian parsley

1 tablespoon sliced green onions

1 tablespoon chopped fresh thyme

PRESENTATION

Extra virgin olive oil

Grated Pecorino Romano cheese

Fried sage leaves or chopped parsley

TO COOK LENTILS: Rinse lentils and put them into a small saucepan. Add enough water to cover by 2 inches. Add whole garlic and thyme sprigs. Bring to a boil over high heat. Decrease heat to medium-low and simmer, uncovered, for 15 minutes or until lentils are partially cooked. They will still be crunchy. Drain and set aside in bowl. Do not remove garlic cloves or thyme sprigs.

TO COOK SAUSAGES: In a large skillet, heat olive oil over high heat until hot. Add onion and garlic and sauté until translucent, 2 minutes. Transfer to bowl of partially cooked lentils. Add sausages to skillet, decrease heat to low and sear until browned on the bottom. Continue cooking and turning until deeply browned on all sides, about 10 minutes. Add onion, garlic and lentils to pan. Stir in broth. Remove half the tomatoes from the can, break them up with your fingers and add them to the sausages. Add ½ cup of the tomato juice. Reserve remaining tomatoes and juice for another use. Bring to a boil, decrease heat and simmer, partially covered, until sausages are cooked through, about 10 minutes.

TO FINISH COOKING: Remove sausages to a plate and cover to keep warm. Continue simmering lentils until they are tender, but retain a little crunch, about 8 minutes. Remove whole garlic cloves and thyme sprigs. Season with ¾ teaspoon salt, or to taste, and pepper to taste. Return sausages to pan and cook until heated through. Recipe may be made ahead and refrigerated at this point, if desired. Reheat on stove top. If sauce is too dry, add a little beef broth. Just before serving, stir in parsley, green onions and thyme.

COUNTDOWN

Up to 2 days ahead
- Cook recipe up to the point of adding parsley, green onions and thyme. Refrigerate covered.

Up to 4 hours ahead
- Fry sage, if using.

Just before serving
- Reheat on stove top and stir in herbs.

TO PLATE: With a slotted spoon, spoon lentils into 4 shallow soup bowls. Spoon over a little of the broth. Slice sausages diagonally into ½-inch slices not quite sliced all the way through, retaining their original shape. Arrange over lentils. Drizzle with olive oil. Grate cheese over the top and garnish with fried sage or chopped parsley.

MAKES 4 SERVINGS

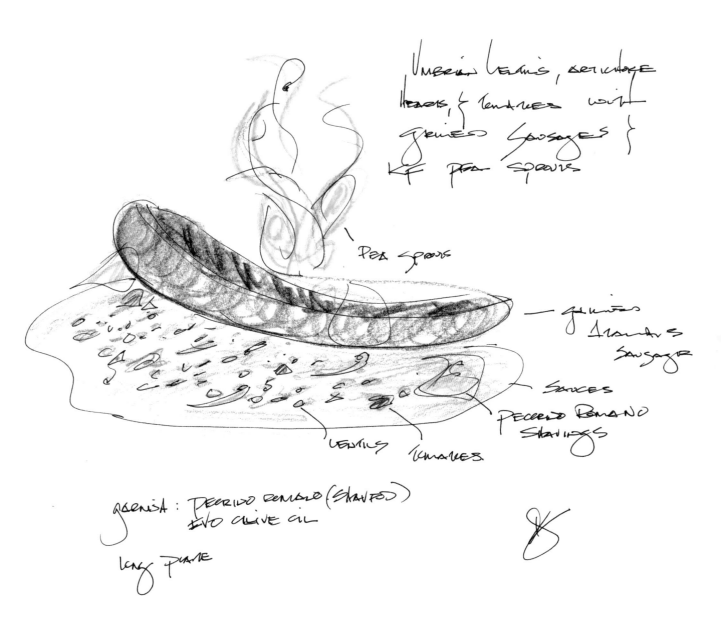

Adobo Pork Ribs
with ono garlic fried rice

I have fond memories of my dad making these ribs when I was growing up. He made the sauce fiery hot by adding a good shaking of sriracha sauce. No matter how spicy he made it, it was never too hot for me. When I make these ribs for my family, I serve them with Ono Garlic Fried Rice. Steamed white rice is good as well.

COUNTDOWN

1 day ahead
• Prepare ribs and refrigerate.

30 minutes ahead
• Make fried rice.
• Reheat ribs.

TIPS:

• At Va de Vi, I split the ribs in half horizontally before cooking to make smaller riblets.

• Like most stews and braised meats, the flavor improves when the ribs are cooked a day ahead. If you have room, refrigerate the ribs in the saucepan they were cooked in. Then all you need to do is put the pan back on the stove and simmer until heated through.

• Chicken thighs can be substituted for the ribs. Cook them until the meat is tender and almost falling off the bone, 30 to 40 minutes.

INGREDIENTS

1 recipe Ono Garlic Fried Rice
   (page 150)
2 tablespoons vegetable oil
1 rack pork spare ribs (about 3 pounds),
   split into 4 portions
6 cloves garlic with peel, smashed
About 6 inches of unpeeled ginger, cut
   into pieces and smashed
3 green onions with tops, cut into
   1-inch pieces
4 star anise
1 tablespoon whole black peppercorns

4 bay leaves
12 sprigs fresh thyme
3 cups unseasoned rice vinegar
1½ cups aji-mirin
1½ cups soy sauce
½ cup superfine sugar

PRESENTATION

Sprigs of cilantro
Bottled sriracha sauce, for
   serving (optional)

TO COOK RIBS: In a large, wide saucepan, such as a Dutch oven, over medium-high heat, heat oil until hot. Sauté ribs in batches until golden brown on both sides, about 5 minutes total; transfer to a bowl. Add garlic, ginger, and green onions to pan and stir-fry until aromatic, 1 minute. Add ribs and stir-fry 2 minutes. Make a bouquet garni by wrapping star anise, peppercorns, bay leaves and thyme in a single layer of cheesecloth like a money bag and tie with string to secure. Add bouquet garni to ribs. In a medium bowl, stir together rice vinegar, aji-mirin, soy sauce and sugar until sugar is dissolved. Pour over ribs to cover. If they are not covered with liquid, transfer to a smaller, deeper pan. Bring to a boil. Decrease heat and simmer, covered, for 60 minutes or until meat is tender and beginning to fall off the bone. Remove bouquet garni. Cut between ribs.

TO PLATE: Spoon a mound of rice onto each plate. Place 3 to 4 ribs on rice. Ladle a small amount of sauce over, not so much that it pools on the plate. Garnish with sprigs of cilantro. Pass sriracha sauce for those with fiery palates.
MAKES 6 SERVINGS

Rioja Braised Beef Short Ribs

with creamy polenta

This recipe is proof that the simplest ingredients can produce spectacular results. The sauce is made by slowly simmering the ribs in Spanish Rioja red wine, beef broth and a mirepoix of chopped vegetables. When the meat is ready to fall off the bone, the vegetables and liquid are pureed to produce an extremely flavorful sauce. Spoon all this over a bed of polenta and watch your friends and family scrape up every last drop.

TIPS:

- The ribs can be eaten immediately after making them, but the flavor improves when made a day ahead.

- You will have an abundant amount of sauce. Leftovers may be used to cook pot roast or beef stew. It can be frozen and used to make a new batch of ribs.

INGREDIENTS

1 recipe Creamy Polenta (page 144)
4 bone-in cross-cut short ribs, cut 3 inches thick and cut crosswise so they are 1½ inches long
6 sprigs fresh thyme, broken in thirds
1 tablespoon black peppercorns
2 bay leaves, torn into pieces
½ cup all-purpose flour
3 tablespoons extra virgin olive oil
1 large onion, chopped

3 carrots, peeled and chopped
3 stalks celery, chopped
1 bottle (750 ml) Rioja wine
4 to 6 tablespoons beef demi-glace dissolved in 2 cups of water
1 can (14 ounces) whole tomatoes in juice

PRESENTATION

Sprigs of Italian parsley

TO PREPARE RIBS: Tie a piece of kitchen string horizontally around the center of each rib to help keep the meat on the bone. Make a bouquet garni by wrapping thyme, peppercorns and bay leaves in one layer of cheesecloth, pull up like a money bag and tie with string to secure. Season both sides of ribs with sea salt and freshly ground pepper. Put flour in a shallow dish and coat both sides of ribs.

TO COOK RIBS: Heat oil in a Dutch oven over high heat until hot. Add ribs and sauté until well browned, turning occasionally, about 10 minutes. Remove ribs to a plate. Add onion, carrots and celery to the pan and sauté until onions are translucent, 2 to 3 minutes. Add ribs to pan. Add the bouquet garni. Pour in the red wine, beef broth and juice from tomatoes. Break up tomatoes with your fingers and add to the pan. If there is not enough liquid to cover ribs by 2 inches, add up to 2 cups of wine, broth or water. Bring to a boil over high heat, decrease heat and simmer the ribs, covered, for 3 hours or until very tender when pierced with a fork.

TO MAKE SAUCE: Transfer ribs to a plate and remove string; cover with foil. Remove bouquet garni; squeeze it to extract the flavor and discard. If available, use an immersion blender to puree. Otherwise, transfer one-third of the sauce to a blender and puree; pour into another pan and repeat with remaining

COUNTDOWN

Up to 2 days ahead

- Cook ribs and puree sauce. If you have room, refrigerate the ribs and sauce in the pan they were cooked in. Cover the surface of the sauce with a piece of waxed paper, cover pan and when cool, refrigerate.

30 minutes ahead

- Reheat ribs in sauce.
- Make polenta.

sauce. Season with sea salt and freshly ground pepper. Add short ribs to sauce. If serving immediately, reheat until hot.

TO PLATE: Spoon polenta into 4 shallow soup bowls. Top each with 2 short ribs. Spoon sauce over the top so that it pools around the polenta. Top with a sprig of parsley.

MAKES 4 SERVINGS

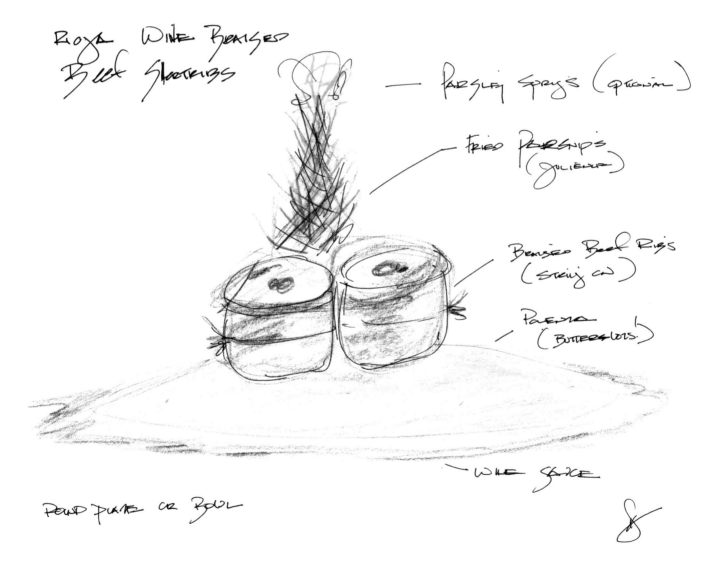

Meatballs and Orchiette
in tomato sauce with basil

Three types of meat and fresh herbs make these meatballs very special. In the restaurant I use trofie pasta, which looks like short pieces of thin, twisted cord. Unfortunately, it is not readily available. If you can't find it, feel free to use any small pasta you like, such as orchiette.

TIPS:

- I've written this recipe following the techniques we use in the restaurant. We cook the pasta about an hour ahead and then reheat it before serving. Of course, you can cook the pasta and serve it immediately if you prefer.
- To get perfectly round meatballs, chill the meat before shaping it.
- These meatballs make great meatball sandwiches.

INGREDIENTS

1 recipe Tomato Sauce with Basil
   (page 160)

MEATBALLS

2 tablespoons plus 3 tablespoons
   olive oil
1 cup finely chopped onions
2 teaspoons finely chopped garlic
2 teaspoons fresh chopped marjoram
2 teaspoons fresh chopped oregano
8 ounces lean ground beef
8 ounces ground veal
8 ounces ground mild sausage

1 large egg
1 teaspoon sea salt
¼ teaspoon freshly ground pepper
¾ cup panko (Japanese bread crumbs)
8 ounces orchiette or other
   small-shaped pasta

PRESENTATION

Chopped chives or parsley
Grated Pecorino Romano cheese

COUNTDOWN

Up to 1 day ahead
- Make meatball mixture and refrigerate covered.
- When meat is cold, shape meatballs and refrigerate covered.
- Make tomato sauce and refrigerate.

1 hour ahead
- Bring tomato sauce to room temperature.
- Coat meatballs in crumbs.
- Cook pasta, drain, run under cold water and cover.

40 minutes ahead
- Sauté meatballs.

15 minutes ahead
- Bake meatballs.

Just before serving
- Reheat pasta in boiling water.
- Reheat tomato sauce until warm.

TO MAKE MEATBALLS: Put 2 tablespoons olive oil, onion and garlic into a large unheated skillet. Turn the heat to medium and cook, stirring, for 1 minute. Decrease heat to low and cook, stirring occasionally, until translucent, about 5 minutes. Stir in marjoram and oregano. Remove from heat and cool slightly. Meanwhile, in a large bowl, mix beef, veal and sausage until combined. Add onion mixture, egg, salt and pepper. Mix until blended. Cover and refrigerate until chilled, 30 minutes or longer. Using a small scoop and your hands, make 1¼- to 1½-inch balls. Put into a shallow baking dish; cover and refrigerate until ready to cook.

TO MAKE PASTA: Cook pasta as package directs, but undercook it slightly because it will cook again. Drain and run under cold water until pasta is cool. Cover and set aside.

TO COOK MEATBALLS: Preheat oven to 350°F. Line a rimmed baking sheet with foil. Put bread crumbs into a pie plate. Roll meatballs in crumbs to coat all sides. Place on baking sheet. Heat 3 tablespoons olive oil in a large skillet over medium heat. The oil is the right temperature when you add a few bread crumbs to it and it bubbles around them. Add half the meatballs to oil. Cook over medium heat, turning, until all sides are golden, about 6 minutes. Return to baking sheet. Cook remaining meatballs in the same manner. Bake meatballs for 15 minutes or until cooked through. If needed, meatballs can stay in oven on off for 30 minutes.

JUST BEFORE SERVING: Bring a large pot of water to a full boil. Add cooked pasta and immediately turn off heat. Reheat tomato sauce briefly; you do not want it to cook. Drain pasta and transfer to a large bowl, add tomato sauce and toss. Season with sea salt and pepper.

TO PLATE: Spoon pasta in the center of 6 small plates. Top each with 4 meatballs. Sprinkle with chives or parsley and grated cheese.

MAKES 6 SERVINGS

Seared Filet Mignon
with morels and farro

Filet mignon steaks are cut from the tenderloin, so they are incredibly tender. Marinating the filets overnight in a gutsy green marinade increases their flavor. It may seem like a lot of marinade for one pound of meat, but in order to do its job, it must cover the meat completely.

TIPS:

- The only time-consuming step in making the marinade is removing the thyme stems from the leaves. If you include the thin, tender stems with the leaves (not the heavy wooden ones) it will save time.
- Black trumpet mushrooms can be substituted for the morels.
- Make sure your skillet is very hot before adding steaks. You want them to caramelize and get crusty on the outside when you sear them.
- If your skillet doesn't have an ovenproof handle, cover it with a double thickness of aluminum foil.

INGREDIENTS

1 recipe Farro with Artichokes and Tomatoes (page 145)
1 recipe Crispy Fried Sage Leaves (page 162)

GARLIC AND THYME MARINADE

1 cup extra virgin olive oil
1 shallot, peeled and quartered
6 cloves garlic, peeled
½ cup thyme leaves (¾ ounces on stems)
1 tablespoon black peppercorns
1 cup parsley leaves
1 dried or fresh bay leaf
6 filet mignon steaks, 1 inch thick (3 to 4 ounces each)
8 to 12 ounces morel mushrooms
1 tablespoon extra virgin olive oil
2 teaspoons finely chopped garlic

PRESENTATION

Porcini oil

COUNTDOWN

Up to 2 days ahead
- Make marinade and refrigerate.

1 day ahead
- Marinate steaks and refrigerate.

Up to 1 day ahead
- Cook and trim artichokes.

Up to 6 hours ahead
- Prepare all ingredients for farro with artichokes and tomatoes.
- Boil farro. Cover and leave at room temperature.

4 hours ahead
- Marinate steaks at room temperature.
- Make fried sage leaves.

Up to 3 hours ahead
- Prepare morels.

Up to 30 minutes ahead
- Finish cooking farro. Cover and leave in warm place.

20 minutes ahead
- Sauté steaks and bake with mushrooms.

TO MAKE MARINADE: Blend all ingredients in a blender until pureed. Use immediately or refrigerate up to 2 days. Bring to room temperature and whisk well before using. Makes 1¼ cups.

TO MARINATE STEAKS: Push each steak together with your fingers to plump it up and make it more cylindrical. Tie a string around the center of the outside edge to help keep its shape. Place steaks in a plastic zipper bag. Pour marinade over, tossing to coat. Refrigerate overnight, turning occasionally. Marinate at room temperature 4 hours before cooking.

TO PREPARE MORELS: Cut the morels in half and brush them to remove any grit or sand. Put them into a bowl and add olive oil and garlic. Season with sea salt and pepper; toss well. Transfer to a shallow pan or deep dish pie plate that can hold them in 2 layers.

TO COOK STEAKS AND MUSHROOMS: Preheat oven to 375°F. Remove steaks from marinade (do not remove marinade clinging to meat) and season with sea salt and pepper. Heat a large skillet over high heat until very hot. Add steaks (they should sizzle and smoke) and sear until bottoms are brown and crusty, about 3 minutes. Turn and brown on other side, 2 more minutes. Transfer skillet to oven. Put mushrooms in oven with steaks. Bake steaks for 5 minutes. A thermometer inserted in center of meat should read 125°F for medium rare. Remove steaks, cover loosely with foil and let rest 10 minutes for juices to settle. Continue baking mushrooms for 5 more minutes or until tender, but not limp, 10 minutes total. Cut strings off steaks.

TO PLATE: Spoon farro and a little juice on the bottom of 6 dinner plates. Top each with a steak. Spoon mushrooms around steak and drizzle with porcini oil. Top with fried sage leaves.

MAKES 6 SERVINGS

Yellowfin Tuna Sashimi

with red tobiko and seaweed salad

In Hawaii there is a tradition of serving tuna sashimi at every celebration. In recognition of this time-honored custom, I felt it was important to include a sashimi recipe in this book.

TIP:

- It is very important to purchase sashimi grade # 1 tuna. If it has any blood or skin on it, remove it before cooking.

INGREDIENTS

1 recipe Soba Noodle Salad
    (page 152)
1 pound sashimi grade #1 tuna in a block
    (7 inches long by 1½ inches wide by
    1 inch thick)

PRESENTATION

Seaweed salad
Pickled ginger
Furikake (nori blend)
Ponzu
Red tobiko

TO PREPARE SASHIMI: Cut tuna in half crosswise, then cut each half into three slices. Cut each slice in half across the grain into 1¼ to 1½ inch thick slices.

TO PLATE: Spoon a small mound of noodle salad on plate. Overlap 2 slices of tuna on top of salad. Top with seaweed salad and pickled ginger. Sprinkle furikake around salad and around plate. Sprinkle with ponzu. Top with a dollop of red tobiko.

MAKES 6 SERVINGS

COUNTDOWN

Up to 4 hours ahead
- Make noodle salad. Do not add ponzu.

30 minutes ahead
- Make sashimi.
- Toss salad with ponzu.

Yellow and Red Beet Salad
with arugula, goat cheese and crispy fried shallots

Some dishes come together like magic. That is how I feel about this combination of sweet red and yellow beets, tangy arugula and salty goat cheese all coated with a spirited Dijon mustard vinaigrette.

TIPS:

* Oven-poach red and yellow beets in one dish so the outside of the yellow beets are tinged with red, which is quite striking.

* At the restaurant, I top this salad with a slice of Bermuda triangle goat cheese from Cyprus Grove Chèvre; it makes a great addition if you can find it.

* To keep your hands from becoming stained when peeling beets, it's a good idea to wear rubber gloves.

INGREDIENTS

½ recipe Dijon Mustard Vinaigrette
   (page 156)
1 recipe Crispy Fried Shallots
   (page 162)
1 red beet (8 ounces)

1 yellow beet (8 ounces)
½ ounce fresh thyme sprigs (about 10)
2 cups baby arugula (about 1 ounce)
2 ounces goat cheese, crumbled
Freshly ground pepper

TO COOK BEETS: Preheat oven to 375°F. Rinse beets, cut off stems and put unpeeled beets into an ovenproof casserole. Add enough water to cover three-quarters of the beets. Add thyme. Cover tightly and bake for 75 to 90 minutes or until tender when pierced with a fork. When cool enough to handle, using a small sharp knife, remove peel. Cool to room temperature.

TO ASSEMBLE SALAD: Cut beets into eight segments. Put into a bowl and toss with 3 tablespoons vinaigrette. Put arugula in another bowl and toss with 1 tablespoon vinaigrette.

TO PLATE: Divide red and yellow beets evenly into shallow soup bowls. Put a handful of arugula in the center. Crumble goat cheese over the top. Grind pepper over to taste. Drizzle a little of the remaining vinaigrette over all. Top with fried shallots.

MAKES 4 SERVINGS

COUNTDOWN

Up to 1 week ahead
* Make mustard vinaigrette and refrigerate.

Up to 1 day ahead
* Cook beets and refrigerate.

Up to 4 hours ahead
* Fry shallots.

1 hour ahead
* Bring vinaigrette and beets to room temperature.

Just before serving
* Assemble salad.

Seared Duck Breasts

with okinawa sweet potato puree, port-scented jus and pear and star anise chutney

Duck has an affinity for anything sweet. In the fall, you may be lucky enough to find Okinawa sweet potatoes in a supermarket. If you are, grab them. Their vivid purple hue and intense sweetness is awesome with the duck. Any sweet potatoes or yams will work well, too. The quick pear chutney adds a nice sweet and sour note to the dish.

TIPS:

- Duck breasts should be served rare or medium rare. If cooked longer, the meat becomes very dry. If using a thermometer, insert it into the side of the breast in the thickest part of the meat; that way you won't disturb the appearance of the skin.
- If your skillet doesn't have an ovenproof handle, cover it with a double thickness of aluminum foil.

COUNTDOWN

Up to 2 days ahead
- Make chutney and refrigerate.

1½ hours ahead
- Marinate duck breasts.
- Prepare all ingredients for sauce.
- Bring chutney to room temperature.
- Make sweet potato puree. Keep covered at room temperature.

20 minutes ahead
- Cook duck breasts.
- Make sauce.
- Reheat sweet potatoes.

INGREDIENTS

1 recipe Pear and Star Anise Chutney (page 165)
1 recipe Okinawa Sweet Potato Puree (page 149)
2 duck breasts (12 to 16 ounces each), Pekin or Muscovy preferred

PORT WINE MARINADE
1 tablespoon finely chopped garlic
1 tablespoon finely chopped shallots
2 tablespoons coarsely chopped thyme (cut right through any soft stems)
2 tablespoons coarsely chopped fresh sage
¼ teaspoon sea salt
2 teaspoons freshly ground pepper
½ teaspoon Chinese five-spice
1 cup ruby port

RUBY PORT SAUCE
¼ cup ruby port
1 teaspoon finely chopped shallots
2 to 3 tablespoons chicken demi-glace dissolved in 1 cup hot water
1 teaspoon chopped fresh thyme
4 tablespoons (½ stick) butter
¼ teaspoon sea salt
¼ teaspoon freshly ground pepper

PRESENTATION
Orange oil
Watercress or sage leaves

TO PREPARE AND MARINATE DUCK: Trim off any excess fat or bone around each breast. Rinse breasts and pat dry. In a bowl, combine marinade ingredients. Add breasts and toss to coat. Marinate at room temperature, meat side down, for 30 to 60 minutes. Turn and marinate 15 to 30 minutes longer.

TO COOK DUCK: Preheat oven to 400°F. Remove duck from marinade and discard marinade. Blot skin side of duck dry. Leave marinade on meat side. Season both sides with sea salt and pepper. Heat large skillet over high heat until very hot, but not smoking. Add duck skin side down and cook until skin is very brown, 3 to 4 minutes. Turn and cook 2 minutes on meat side. Transfer skillet to oven. Bake for 5 to 7 minutes or until a meat thermometer inserted into the thickest part of the meat reads 120°F for rare, 130°F for medium rare. They will continue to cook when taken out of the oven. Remove breasts from pan and cover them with foil.

TO MAKE SAUCE: Pour fat from skillet. Wipe pan clean. Add port, shallots and broth. Cook over high heat until reduced to about ⅔ cup. Stir in thyme, butter, salt and pepper. Stir until butter melts. Remove from heat.

TO PLATE: Slice breasts diagonally into ⅜-inch-thick slices. Spoon a dollop of sweet potatoes into center of 4 small plates. Fan slices of duck off center over half the potatoes. Spoon sauce on plate around duck and then drizzle lightly over duck. Top with a dollop of chutney and drizzle with orange oil. Garnish with watercress or sage leaves.

MAKES 4 SERVINGS

Toasted Macadamia Nut Cream Tartlet

These decadent tartlets with their buttery cookie crust and macadamia custard filling are a salute to my Hawaiian heritage.

TIPS:

- You will need four 4 ½-inch-tartlet tins with removable bottoms.
- I use sweet pastry for tarts because it doesn't shrink like regular pie dough and doesn't need to be blind baked.
- If you have a convection oven, use it to bake the crusts; decrease oven temperature to 350°F.
- Macadamia nuts may be chopped in a food processor or with a sharp knife.
- A toaster oven is great for toasting nuts.

INGREDIENTS

1 recipe Chocolate Sauce (page 154)
1 recipe Caramel Sauce (page 154)
¾ cup chopped macadamia nuts, toasted, divided

SWEET PASTRY

¾ cup (1½ sticks) butter, at room temperature
⅔ cup powdered sugar
2 cups all-purpose flour
Pinch of sea salt

PASTRY CREAM

1½ cups whole milk
One 3-inch vanilla bean
4 egg yolks
¼ cup sugar
3 tablespoons all-purpose flour

PRESENTATION

¾ cup whipping cream, whipped with 1 tablespoon powdered sugar
Reserved ¼ cup toasted macadamia nuts

COUNTDOWN

Up to 4 days ahead
- Make chocolate and caramel sauces.

Up to 2 days ahead
- Make pastry dough and refrigerate.
- Make pastry cream and refrigerate.

Up to 8 hours ahead
- Roll pastry, fit into tins and bake. Leave at room temperature.

Up to 6 hours ahead
- Fill tartlets, decorate with whipped cream and nuts; refrigerate.

20 minutes before serving
- Bring tartlets to room temperature.

TO TOAST NUTS: Toast chopped nuts at 325°F until lightly golden in color.

TO MAKE PASTRY: In a mixing bowl with electric beaters, mix butter and powdered sugar until blended. Add flour and mix until pastry holds together and begins to form a ball, scraping sides as needed. Remove to a work surface and shape into a flat round. Cut into 4 equal portions. Wrap in plastic wrap and refrigerate for at least 1 hour.

TO MAKE PASTRY CREAM: Pour milk into a medium saucepan, preferably nonstick. Slice vanilla bean lengthwise down the center, scrape the seeds into the milk and add the bean. Stir to distribute. Bring milk to a simmer over medium-low heat until it is hot and begins to steam. Meanwhile, in a mixing bowl with a whisk or electric mixer, mix egg yolks and sugar until thick and light colored. Mix in flour. While mixing, pour a little hot milk into yolk mixture to heat it. Add the warmed yolks to the heated milk and cook, stirring constantly with a wooden spoon, until cream comes to a boil. Remove from heat and press through a strainer into a bowl. Stir in ½ cup macadamia nuts. Cool to room temperature. Cover snugly with plastic wrap and refrigerate until cold.

TO ROLL PASTRY: Place oven rack in lower third of oven and preheat oven to 375°F. Remove pastry from refrigerator and leave at room temperature for 10 minutes or until soft enough to roll. It must still be very cold. Roll one piece of dough between 2 sheets of parchment paper into a circle that is about ¼ inch thick. Remove top parchment paper. Place pastry round over top of tin and remove second sheet of parchment. Gently press pastry into bottom and up sides of tin. Fold the sides down so they are thicker than the bottom. If dough tears, it is easy to fix by pressing in a small piece of dough. Remove excess pastry so it is even with the rim of the tins.

TO BAKE: Place tins on a baking sheet. Bake at 375°F for 15 to 17 minutes or until pastry is pale golden. Remove from oven and cool to room temperature.

TO ASSEMBLE AND PLATE: Spread pastry cream into tart shells. Pipe whipped cream through a star tip or dollop with a spoon around the outer rims. Sprinkle reserved ¼ cup macadamia nuts into the centers. Remove sides of tins and, if desired, remove bottom by slipping a small knife into one edge and lifting tart up. Place on a baking sheet and refrigerate until serving. Bring to room temperature 20 minutes before serving. Garnish the plates with ribbons of chocolate and caramel sauces and place tartlets in the center.

MAKES 4 TARTLETS

Sides, Sauces and Garnishes

sides

Beefsteak Tomato Sorbet

This frosty sorbet has so many layers of taste that it can almost be compared to a good wine. When it first hits your palate you'll taste the sweetness of tomatoes, then the zing of sherry vinegar, ending with a note of pepper. It is delicious served with a summer salad like my Parma Prosciutto-Wrapped Ambrosia Melon (page 83). It makes a good intermezzo course, and it's also refreshing eaten right out of the freezer.

COUNTDOWN

Up to 3 weeks ahead
• Make sugar syrup and refrigerate.

Up to 1 week ahead
• Make and freeze sorbet.

INGREDIENTS
SUGAR SYRUP
1½ cups sugar
1½ cups water

TOMATO SORBET
2 pounds very ripe beefsteak tomatoes

3 tablespoons lemon juice plus 1 tablespoon lemon juice
3 tablespoons sherry vinegar
2 tablespoons kosher salt
1 tablespoon freshly ground pepper

TO MAKE SUGAR SYRUP: Put sugar and water into a small saucepan. Bring to a simmer over medium heat, stirring occasionally. Simmer until sugar is dissolved, about 4 minutes. Cool to room temperature. Syrup can be used immediately or refrigerated.

TO MAKE SORBET: Core and peel tomatoes and cut them into chunks. Put one-third into a blender container. Add 3 tablespoons lemon juice, vinegar, salt and pepper. Blend until pureed. Transfer to a bowl. Blend remaining tomatoes in 2 batches. Add to bowl. Stir in sugar syrup. Taste, and if desired, add more lemon juice. Refrigerate until chilled. Freeze in an ice cream machine according to manufacturer's directions. It will take approximately 50 minutes and will not freeze firm. Transfer to a freezer container and freeze. It will firm up enough to make perfect scoops.

MAKES 1 QUART

Creamed Corn

When corn is cooked in flavored cream with garlic and red onion, it makes an absolutely delicious side dish. Serve it with meat, poultry and fish, such as the Grilled Wild Alaskan Salmon (page 82) and Grilled Skirt Steaks (page 106).

COUNTDOWN

Up to 1 day ahead
• Make the corn cream and refrigerate.

Just before serving
• Finish creamed corn.

TIPS:

• Be careful not to overcook the corn or it will lose flavor and texture. Much of the appeal of this dish lies in the fresh corn retaining some crunch.

• When the dish is finished, the corn will continue to absorb the cream and thicken. If not serving immediately, remove from the heat while the sauce is still runny. If it gets too thick, thin with a little cream or milk.

INGREDIENTS

CORN CREAM
2 ears fresh corn on the cob
½ cup whole milk
1 cup heavy cream

CREAMED CORN
2 tablespoons butter
1 teaspoon finely chopped garlic

2 tablespoons finely chopped red onion
2 tablespoons sliced green onions, with tops
¼ teaspoon sea salt

PRESENTATION
Julienned fresh chervil or Italian parsley

TO MAKE CORN CREAM: Cut corn off cobs and reserve corn. You should have about 2 cups. Cut cobs in half and put them into a small saucepan that will hold them in one layer. Add milk and cream. Simmer uncovered over medium heat for 20 to 25 minutes, or until cream has reduced to ⅔ cup. Watch carefully that it doesn't boil over. Strain into a bowl; discard cobs. Cream may be used immediately or refrigerated.

TO MAKE CREAMED CORN: In a 10-inch skillet over medium heat, melt butter. Add garlic and red onion. Cook, stirring, until translucent, 2 minutes. Add corn and cook, stirring, until coated with butter. Stir in corn cream. Bring to a boil over medium heat, stirring occasionally, until thickened slightly, 2 to 3 minutes. Do not overcook or sauce will separate. Stir in green onions and salt; pepper to taste. Taste, and if not sweet enough, add a small amount of sugar. If not serving immediately, corn will continue to absorb the cream and the sauce will thicken.

TO PLATE: Garnish with fresh chervil or parsley.

MAKES 4 TO 5 SERVINGS

Creamy Polenta

You won't find any cream in this polenta. Butter is the secret that makes it rich and creamy.

TIP:

- Polenta takes 25 minutes of stirring which might be difficult if your guests aren't in the kitchen with you. When made ahead, it will become very thick. Simply stir in a little water and reheat it. It is best made as close to serving as possible.

INGREDIENTS

3½ cups water
1 teaspoon sea salt plus ¾ teaspoon sea salt
¾ cup polenta

6 tablespoons (⅔ stick) unsalted butter, at room temperature
½ teaspoon freshly ground pepper

TO MAKE POLENTA: In a wide saucepan over high heat, bring water and 1 teaspoon salt to a boil. Sprinkle polenta over the top, stirring constantly to distribute it. Lower heat to medium and continue boiling, stirring constantly and making sure the bottom doesn't stick, until the mixture begins to thicken. Decrease heat to medium-low and simmer, stirring and scraping the bottom, until polenta is as thick as mashed potatoes and pulls away from the sides of the pan, about 25 minutes. It should be tender but retain a little bit of crunch. Cut butter into pieces and stir into polenta. Season with remaining ¾ teaspoon sea salt and pepper.

MAKES 4 SERVINGS

Exotic Mushroom Ragout

I like to use an assortment of three or four types of mushrooms in this dish. My favorites are gamboni, alba, oyster and shiitake, but feel free to experiment. This versatile recipe complements a myriad of entrees: pork, beef, poultry or fish. I use it as a side dish and in the gravy to make Pan-Fried Kurobuta Pork Chops (page 96) and in the beef jus in Grilled Skirt Steaks (page 106).

COUNTDOWN

Up to 1 day ahead
- Make ragout and refrigerate.

Just before serving
- Reheat in a saucepan on the stove.

TIP:

- The recipe yields enough for 4 small plates. If desired, it can be doubled in the same size skillet.

INGREDIENTS

2 tablespoons extra virgin olive oil
2 tablespoons coarsely chopped shallots

8 ounces assorted mushrooms, cleaned and sliced, if large
¼ cup dry white wine, such as sauvignon blanc

TO MAKE RAGOUT: In a 12-inch skillet over medium-high heat, heat oil until hot. Add shallots and sauté until lightly browned, 1 minute. Add mushrooms and sauté, stirring constantly, until they soften slightly and are reduced in size, 2 to 3 minutes. Add wine and boil, stirring occasionally, until wine is reduced to 2 tablespoons, about 2 minutes. Remove from heat before mushrooms turn limp. Season with sea salt and pepper.

MAKES 4 SERVINGS

Farro with Artichokes and Tomatoes

Farro is an ancient Tuscan grain with a mellow, nutty flavor. It is cooked in boiling water, like pasta, until al dente. It can be eaten plain, used in a salad or stirred into a sauce. When customers who are not familiar with farro order this dish, they are so surprised and delighted with the taste that they almost always place a second order.

COUNTDOWN

Up to 1 day ahead
• Prepare artichoke hearts.

Up to 6 hours ahead
• Boil farro and prep all ingredients. Cover and leave at room temperature.

Up to 4 hours ahead
• Make fried sage leaves.

15 minutes ahead
• Stir-fry and complete farro.

INGREDIENTS

1 recipe Fresh Artichokes (page 146)
1 recipe Crispy Fried Sage Leaves (page 162)
1 cup uncooked whole grain farro (sometimes labeled as perlato, semiperlato, or decorticato)
1 can (14 ounces) whole tomatoes in juice

2 tablespoons extra virgin olive oil
1 tablespoon finely chopped garlic
1 tablespoon chopped shallots
½ cup chopped mushrooms
1 tablespoon chopped fresh sage
1¼ cups hot beef or vegetable broth, divided
½ teaspoon sea salt
¼ teaspoon freshly ground pepper

TO COOK FARRO: Bring a medium pot of salted water to a boil over high heat. Add farro and return to a boil. Reduce heat to medium and boil slowly, uncovered, for 15 minutes. Farro should be a little firmer than al dente, but not completely done because it will be cooked a second time. Drain and transfer to a bowl.

TO STIR-FRY AND COMPLETE COOKING: Remove tomatoes from juice and put them into a bowl. Don't drain them because you want a little juice clinging to them. Squeeze tomatoes with your fingers to coarsely break them up and set aside. In a large skillet, heat olive oil over medium heat until hot. Add garlic, shallots, mushrooms and sage. Sauté for 2 minutes or until aromatic. Add farro and sauté 2 minutes. Stir in 1 cup hot broth. Reduce heat to medium-low and cook, stirring, until most of the liquid is absorbed. Add artichoke hearts, crushed tomatoes and remaining ¼ cup broth. Simmer, stirring occasionally, until farro is tender but retains a little crunch and there is enough liquid to coat the bottom of the pan, about 10 minutes. Season with sea salt and pepper. If it needs to be held, be sure there is lots of extra liquid in the pan. It will continue to absorb it as it sits. If it becomes too dry, add a little hot broth or water.

TO PLATE: Spoon farro into shallow soup bowls and top with fried sage leaves.

MAKES 6 TO 8 SERVINGS

Fresh Artichokes

I always cook artichokes whole, even when I only need the hearts for a dish, like Farro with Artichokes and Tomatoes (page 145). The edible parts of the leaves are delicious dipped in melted butter or mayonnaise.

COUNTDOWN

Up to 1 day ahead
* Prepare artichokes and refrigerate hearts overnight.

TIPS:
* Soak artichokes in lemon water before cooking to help tenderize and bring out their flavor.
* A globe artichoke is the typical artichoke found in supermarkets.

INGREDIENTS

2 medium to large globe artichokes   1 lemon, cut in half

TO PREPARE ARTICHOKES: Working with one artichoke at a time, tear off the tough bottom leaves closest to the stem and discard. Cut off bottom ¼ inch of stem. With scissors, snip off the tips of the leaves that have sharp thorns. Turn the artichoke on its side; with a serrated knife, slice off the top of the leaves. Fill a large, deep non-aluminum pot three-fourths full of water. Squeeze juice from lemon into water and add lemon halves. Add artichokes. Cover with a plate to keep artichokes under the water. Set aside to soak at room temperature for at least 30 minutes or as long as overnight.

TO COOK: Bring artichokes to a boil over high heat with the plate still on them to keep them submerged. Boil over medium heat for 30 to 45 minutes or until an interior leaf can be pulled off easily and is tender. Drain and run under cold water to stop the cooking.

TO TRIM ARTICHOKES FOR HEARTS: Peel all large leaves from artichokes. Reserve for another use. Discard all thin and purple-tinged leaves. With a teaspoon, scoop out the fuzzy choke. Using a small, sharp knife, peel stem. You will be left with a scooped-out heart (sometimes referred to as the bottom) attached to the stem. It can be used whole, chopped or sliced.

Fresh Ratatouille

Traditional ratatouille is a mixture of vegetables cooked until they become so limp they are unrecognizable. I cook each vegetable individually, so they retain their fresh, crisp texture. I then toss them with a fragrant splash of balsamic vinegar. It is as important to use good quality balsamic vinegar as it is to use good olive oil. You can't get great results with inferior products. Would you use 25-year-old balsamic vinegar to brighten the flavor of vegetables? Some aficionados might. I guess it depends on how much you like ratatouille.

COUNTDOWN

Up to 5 hours ahead
• Salt and drain eggplant.

Up to 4 hours ahead
• Cook vegetables. Cover and keep at room temperature.

Just before serving
• Finish ratatouille.

INGREDIENTS

1 pound eggplant
¾ teaspoon sea salt
1 pound bell peppers, yellow and red preferred
½ pound zucchini
½ pound yellow summer squash, such as crookneck or sunburst
6 tablespoons extra virgin olive oil, divided

1 pound yellow onions, diced
3 teaspoons plus 2 tablespoons finely chopped garlic
¾ cup toy box or grape tomatoes
2 tablespoons balsamic vinegar
3 tablespoons julienned fresh basil

PRESENTATION

Julienned basil

TO PREPARE VEGETABLES: Peel eggplant and cut into ½-inch cubes. Put in a colander in the sink and sprinkle with 1 teaspoon sea salt. Let drain for one hour. Rinse and dry well. Meanwhile, chop peppers, zucchini and yellow squash into ½-inch cubes; place each in separate bowls. Prepare onions, garlic and tomatoes and place in separate bowls.

TO COOK VEGETABLES: In a large skillet, preferably nonstick, over medium-high heat, heat 1 tablespoon olive oil until hot. Add onions and sauté for 4 to 5 minutes until translucent. Transfer to a large bowl. Add 1 tablespoon oil, 1 teaspoon garlic and eggplant to skillet. Sauté until tender, 5 to 7 minutes. Salt and pepper lightly; transfer to large bowl with onions. Heat 1 tablespoon oil. Add 1 teaspoon garlic and peppers and sauté until tender, but still crisp, about 3 minutes. Transfer to large bowl. Heat 1 tablespoon oil. Add 1 teaspoon garlic and zucchini and yellow squash. Sauté for 2 minutes or until softened slightly. Transfer to large bowl. Vegetables may be held covered at this point.

TO FINISH RATATOUILLE: In same skillet, heat 2 tablespoons oil over high heat until hot and almost smoking. Stir in vegetables and 2 tablespoons garlic. Reduce heat to medium and simmer, stirring, until hot, 2 minutes. Stir in tomatoes until heated through, 2 minutes. Stir in balsamic vinegar and basil. Season with sea salt and pepper.

TO PLATE: Top each serving with julienned basil.

MAKES 8 SIDE DISH SERVINGS

Green Papaya Salad

In the restaurant, I serve a small portion of this salad as a bed under Grilled Kalbi Flat Iron Steak (page 72), Hoisin-Glazed Baby Back Pork Ribs (page 74), and Grilled Pork Satay (page 46). Its sweet, tangy, salty taste and crunchy texture pair well with robust and spicy entrées. To serve as a salad course, spoon it over shredded Napa cabbage or iceberg lettuce. This recipe makes a large quantity.

COUNTDOWN

Up to 4 hours ahead
• Make salad and dressing; refrigerate separately.

Just before serving
• Combine salad and dressing; toss well.

TIPS:

• If you can find a small green papaya, or don't mind using only half of one, you may want to cut the recipe in half.

• Shred papaya in a food processor or by hand on a coarse grater. Make the shreds as long as possible.

• For appearance and texture, add small sprigs of cilantro rather than chopped.

INGREDIENTS

SALAD

1 green papaya, about 2½ pounds, peeled and shredded

1½ cups cilantro sprigs

1½ cups peeled and shredded carrots (about 2 large)

2 green onions with tops, julienned

DRESSING

½ cup fish sauce (nuoc mam)

¼ cup lime juice

½ cup unseasoned rice vinegar

¼ cup superfine sugar

1 teaspoon chili sauce with garlic

¼ cup julienned mint

¼ cup chopped cilantro

TO MAKE DRESSING: In a small bowl, whisk all ingredients.

TO MAKE SALAD: In a large bowl, toss all ingredients together. Just before serving, add dressing to salad and toss well.

MAKES 9 CUPS SALAD

Kimchee

Kimchee is a fiery hot Korean condiment made by pickling shredded cabbage. This is an American version that is toned down considerably. You can make it as hot as you like by increasing the jarred liquid kimchee base. For more complex heat, add chili sauce with garlic or sriracha sauce. Kimchee is easy to make, but purchased kimchee can be substituted.

COUNTDOWN

Up to 1 week ahead
• Make kimchee and refrigerate.

TIP:

• When the cabbage is first shredded you will have about 9 cups. After it soaks in salt water overnight, it shrinks down to about 5 cups.

INGREDIENTS

1 head Napa cabbage (about
   1½ pounds)
2 tablespoons plus ½ teaspoon sea salt
1 cup unseasoned rice vinegar

¼ cup superfine sugar
2 tablespoons jarred liquid kimchee
   base, or to taste

TO PREPARE CABBAGE: Discard outer leaves of cabbage. Cut 3 inches off bottom, separate leaves and rinse them. Cut out hard white core on each leaf. Pile leaves up and thinly slice them. You should have about 9 cups. Put cabbage into a large bowl. Add 10 cups of water and 2 tablespoons salt. Stir until salt dissolves. Cover and set aside at room temperature overnight.

TO FINISH KIMCHEE: Drain leaves in a colander in the sink and rinse several times. Return to bowl and add vinegar, sugar, ½ teaspoon salt and kimchee base. Stir well. Refrigerate covered for several hours or up to 1 week, stirring occasionally.

MAKES ABOUT 5 CUPS

Okinawa Sweet Potato Puree

These beautiful purple spuds from Japan are really special. They have a depth of color and sweetness that you'll love. But until they are readily available in our supermarkets, any yam or sweet potato may be substituted. This recipe makes enough for four average servings. If you want to offer seconds, I suggest you increase the recipe.

COUNTDOWN

Up to 2 hours ahead
• Make puree and keep covered in a warm place. Reheat slowly, stirring, over low heat.

INGREDIENTS

1 pound sweet potatoes or yams,
   peeled and cut into chunks
¼ cup reserved potato water

4 tablespoons (½ stick) butter,
   at room temperature
½ teaspoon sea salt
¼ teaspoon freshly ground pepper

TO MAKE PUREE: Put potatoes into a saucepan and add water to cover. Bring to a boil over high heat, decrease heat to medium and boil for 5 to 10 minutes or until tender when pierced with a fork. Place a strainer over a bowl and drain potatoes, reserving water. Return potatoes to pan and mash with a potato masher or back of a wooden spoon. Stir in ¼ cup potato water, butter, salt and pepper. Stir until smooth.

MAKES 4 SERVINGS

Ono Garlic Fried Rice

In Hawaiian, ono means delicious and I think that is a fitting name for this flavorful, yet simple dish. The rice is cooked until the bottom is golden and crusty, the way fried rice is always cooked in China. I call the American version soggy fried rice. This makes a delicious entrée as well as a side dish.

TIP:

- To get 4 cups cooked rice, cook 1½ cups raw jasmine rice according to package directions.

INGREDIENTS

SCRAMBLED EGGS

4 eggs
1 tablespoon vegetable oil
⅓ cup thinly sliced green onions
    with tops

RICE

2 tablespoons vegetable oil

2 Chinese sausages, diced
    (about ⅓ cup)
1 tablespoon finely chopped garlic
4 cups cooked jasmine rice
1 tablespoon soy sauce
1 tablespoon oyster sauce

TO SCRAMBLE EGGS: Stir eggs with a fork until blended. In a 12-inch skillet, preferably non-stick, heat oil over medium-high heat until hot. Add eggs. Sprinkle green onions over. Stir gently with a silicone rubber spatula or wooden spoon until lightly scrambled. Transfer to a bowl.

TO COOK FRIED RICE: Heat oil in the same skillet over high heat until very hot, about 2 minutes. Add sausage and garlic. Stir-fry for 15 to 30 seconds, or until aromatic. Add rice and cook, stirring to break up kernels, until rice begins to brown on bottom, about 8 minutes. Add soy and oyster sauce. Stir and toss until mixed. Add eggs, breaking them up with a spoon as you stir. Continue to cook until some of the kernels are golden and crispy. Serve immediately. If necessary, gently reheat in skillet.

MAKES 6 TO 8 SERVINGS

COUNTDOWN

Just before serving
- Make fried rice.

At Va de Vi, our guest checks are presented in old books. To our delight (and surprise), our guests autograph the inside covers with messages about their dining experience.

Potato Croquettes

Here I take chilled mashed potatoes, add an egg and seasonings, shape them into patties, coat them in bread crumbs and pan fry them to golden goodness. Mashed potatoes with a crispy crust—what could be better?

COUNTDOWN

Up to one day ahead
- Make mashed potatoes; refrigerate at least 2 hours.
- Make croquettes and refrigerate.

TIP:
- If your skillet doesn't have an ovenproof handle, cover it with a double thickness of aluminum foil.

INGREDIENTS

½ recipe Yukon Gold Mashed Potatoes (page 153), refrigerated at least 2 hours
1 egg
1 tablespoon furikake (nori blend)
¼ teaspoon shichimi togarashi (Japanese seven-spice)
¼ cup thinly-sliced green onions with tops
2 cups panko (Japanese bread crumbs)
4 tablespoons olive oil

TO MAKE CROQUETTES: In a medium bowl, stir chilled potatoes and egg until blended. Add furikake, togarashi and green onions. Stir until well blended. Put panko crumbs into a shallow dish. Using an ice cream scoop, scoop 6 balls of potato onto crumbs. With your hands, press into crumbs and shape into patties. Make sure both sides of patties are coated with crumbs. Croquettes may be cooked immediately or refrigerated as long as overnight.

TO COOK CROQUETTES: Preheat oven to 375°F. In a large skillet, heat olive oil over high heat until hot. Add patties and cook until golden on the bottom, 2 to 3 minutes. Turn and brown other side, 2 more minutes. Put skillet in oven and bake for 5 to 10 minutes or until heated through.

MAKES 6 CROQUETTES

Soba Noodle Salad

This is a great salad for a party. It can be easily doubled and by adding slices of cooked pork, chicken or duck, it becomes a savory entrée. In the restaurant, we make the salad with cha soba noodles that are made with green tea and can be found in Asian markets.

COUNTDOWN

Up to 4 hours ahead
• Cook noodles, toss with sesame oil and refrigerate.

Up to 2 hours ahead
• Prep carrots and green onions. Cover and refrigerate.

I hour ahead
• Complete salad and leave at room temperature. If too dry, add more ponzu.

TIP:

• The easiest way to julienne a carrot is on the julienne blade of a mandolin. If you shred the carrot, the salad will have a different texture.

INGREDIENTS

4 ounces dried soba noodles
   (one-half of an 8-ounce package)
2 teaspoons sesame oil
1 package (3½ ounces)
   enoki mushrooms
2 green onions
1 medium carrot, peeled and julienned
   (1 cup)
2 teaspoons toasted sesame seeds
¼ cup bottled ponzu sauce

TO COOK NOODLES: Cook as directed on package. Drain, run under cold water to stop the cooking and drain again. When cool, transfer noodles to a bowl. Add sesame oil and toss to coat. Refrigerate until ready to serve.

TO FINISH SALAD: Cut 1½ inches off mushrooms, break them up and add to noodles. Cut 1 inch off top of green onions and discard. Cut green onions with tops into 2-inch lengths. Slice each piece into thin slivers. Add green onions, carrots and sesame seeds. Toss and add ponzu. Toss until mixed well. Serve at room temperature.

MAKES 4 SERVINGS

Yukon Gold Mashed Potatoes

When my kids were little they always wanted to cook with me, so I taught them how to make mashed potatoes. They are quite adept at it now, and if they can do it, so can any adult. You may be surprised at the amount of butter I use, but these mashed potatoes are so delicious that everyone will ask for the recipe. You'll have to decide if you want to share the butter secret.

COUNTDOWN

Up to 4 hours ahead
• Make potatoes; cover in the pan on the stove and leave at room temperature. Reheat gently before serving.

TIPS:
• For creamy mashed potatoes, they must be mashed while they are hot.
• I prefer mashed potatoes that are slightly lumpy, so I suggest you don't over-mash them.

INGREDIENTS

2 pounds Yukon Gold potatoes, peeled and quartered
1/2 cup reserved potato water

1/4 pound (1 stick) unsalted butter, at room temperature
3/4 teaspoon sea salt

TO MAKE MASHED POTATOES: Put potatoes into a medium saucepan and add enough water to cover by one inch. Bring to a boil over high heat. Decrease heat to medium-high and boil for 20 to 30 minutes or until very soft when pierced with a skewer or knife. Timing will depend on size of potatoes. Place a colander over a bowl and drain, reserving water. Put potatoes back into pan and mash with a wooden spoon or potato masher until lumpy. Add 1/2 cup potato water, butter, 3/4 teaspoon salt and pepper to taste. Mash again until creamy with a few lumps.

VARIATIONS:

WASABI MASHED POTATOES: Stir 1 teaspoon wasabi paste into mashed potatoes.

TRUFFLE MASHED POTATOES: Stir 4 teaspoons black truffle oil into mashed potatoes.

MAKES 6 TO 8 SERVINGS

Sauces and Dressings

Caramel Sauce

I can come up with dozens of uses for this sauce; it's great on ice cream, pies, tarts, cakes and fruit. My son, Keenan, likes it on a spoon right out of the bowl.

COUNTDOWN

Up to 4 hours ahead
• Make sauce and refrigerate.

INGREDIENTS
1½ cups granulated sugar
½ cup water

1 cup heavy whipping cream

TO MAKE SAUCE: In a medium saucepan, preferably not dark so you can see the color of the sugar, bring sugar and water to a boil over medium heat, stirring until sugar is dissolved. Boil, without stirring, until sugar turns mahogany, about 5 minutes. When it begins turning brown, it is alright to stir again. Watch carefully, as it goes from mahogany to burnt very quickly. Remove saucepan from heat and carefully stir in a few tablespoons of cream. The caramel will bubble; when it subsides, add a few more tablespoons of cream. Slowly add the rest of the cream, stirring until smooth. Serve warm or at room temperature. To reheat, microwave on low or heat in a double boiler.

MAKES 1½ CUPS

Chocolate Sauce

This is a rich, ultra-creamy, dark sauce. To match the Toasted Macadamia Nut Cream Tartlet (page 138) photo, pour it and the caramel sauce into separate squirt bottles and pipe them onto the plate around tartlets.

COUNTDOWN

Up to 4 hours ahead
• Make sauce and refrigerate. Reheat before serving.

INGREDIENTS
¾ cup water
¾ cup sugar
¼ cup corn syrup

¾ cup unsweetened cocoa powder
4 ounces semi-sweet
   chocolate, chopped

TO MAKE SAUCE: In a medium saucepan over medium-high heat, bring water, sugar and corn syrup to a boil, stirring until sugar dissolves. Whisk in cocoa powder and return to a boil. Remove from heat and add chocolate. Whisk until melted and smooth. Serve warm.

MAKES 1¼ CUPS

Citrus Butter Sauce

A close relative of a French buerre blanc, the following sauce with its variations begins by reducing wine and flavorings, adding and reducing cream, and finally, whisking in butter. Rich and delicious, it's easy to vary by changing the seasonings and wine and adding fresh herbs.

COUNTDOWN

Up to 2 hours ahead
• Make sauce up to the point of adding butter. Cover and keep at room temperature.

Just before serving
• Finish sauce.

TIPS:

• Completed sauce can be held a few minutes by putting the bowl into a warm water bath.

• If not serving immediately, put sauce in a warm place for up to 30 minutes. If it gets too hot, it will break down; if too cold, it will harden.

INGREDIENTS

1 large shallot, peeled and sliced
6 stems fresh thyme
1 bay leaf
1½ cups dry white wine, such as sauvignon blanc

1 tablespoon grated lemon peel (from 1 large lemon)
½ cup heavy cream
¼ pound (1 stick) unsalted butter, cut into 9 pieces
½ teaspoon sea salt

TO MAKE SAUCE: In a small non-aluminum saucepan over medium heat, bring shallot, thyme, bay leaf, wine and lemon peel to a slow boil. Decrease heat to medium-low and boil slowly, stirring occasionally, until reduced by half, about 10 minutes. Whisk in cream. Simmer, stirring occasionally, until reduced by about one-third to 1 scant cup, 7 to 10 minutes. Pour through a fine mesh strainer into a small bowl. Sauce may be held covered for 2 hours.

TO FINISH SAUCE: Return to saucepan and reheat on low. Add 3 pieces of butter to hot sauce, whisking until incorporated. Whisk in remaining butter, 3 pieces at a time, incorporating each batch before adding the next. Stir in salt; add pepper to taste.

VARIATIONS:

CHERVIL OR CHIVE BUTTER SAUCE: Stir 2 tablespoons chopped fresh chervil into sauce. If fresh chervil is not available, substitute chopped chives.

SAKE-WASABI BUTTER SAUCE: Substitute 1½ cups sake for the dry white wine. Stir 2 teaspoons wasabi paste into the completed sauce.

MAKES 1 CUP

Dijon Mustard Vinaigrette

COUNTDOWN

Up to 3 days ahead
• Make vinaigrette and refrigerate.

I use this thick, zesty vinaigrette for the Niçoise Salad (page 70) and the Yellow and Red Beet Salad (page 134), but don't stop there. It is terrific with roast chicken, grilled or poached fish, roast pork, cooked asparagus, green beans and potato salad. I could go on and on, but if you have leftovers in your refrigerator, I know you will find uses for this vinaigrette I've probably never considered.

TIP:

• If you wish to make half a recipe, make it in a blender. It is too small an amount for a standard food processor.

INGREDIENTS

2 tablespoons plus 1 teaspoon Dijon mustard	3 tablespoons fresh lemon juice
2 shallots, peeled and quartered (¼ cup chopped)	1 cup extra virgin olive oil
	1 teaspoon sea salt
2 tablespoons red wine vinegar	¼ teaspoon freshly ground pepper
	1 tablespoon finely chopped chives

TO PREPARE VINAIGRETTE: In a food processor or blender, process mustard, shallots, vinegar and lemon juice until mixed. With motor running, slowly pour olive oil through the feed tube until mixture is thick and emulsified, about 1 minute. If using a blender, put a towel over the top to keep from spattering. Mix in salt and pepper. Remove to bowl and stir in chives. Use immediately or refrigerate. Bring to room temperature and stir well before using.

MAKES 1⅓ CUPS

Hoisin Barbecue Sauce

COUNTDOWN

Up to 2 weeks ahead
• Make sauce and refrigerate.

Nothing that comes in a bottle compares to this intensely flavored Asian sauce. Slather it on Hoisin-Glazed Baby Back Ribs (page 74), Hoisin-Glazed Lamb Chops (page 94), steaks and pork tenderloin.

TIP:

• This makes more barbecue sauce than needed for one recipe, but it is so versatile that it doesn't make sense to cut it in half.

INGREDIENTS

½ cup hoisin sauce	1 tablespoon packed golden brown sugar
½ cup oyster sauce	
½ cup plum sauce	1 tablespoon chili sauce with garlic
½ cup soy sauce	1 tablespoon freshly grated ginger
½ cup peanut oil	
½ cup honey	1 teaspoon Chinese five-spice

TO PREPARE SAUCE: Whisk all ingredients in a large bowl. Store in refrigerator. Bring to room temperature before using.

MAKES 3¼ CUPS

Homemade Mayonnaise

I like homemade mayonnaise because the flavor is so bright and fresh. By adding herbs and spices, it is easy to turn it into a brand new sauce. Two of my favorite variations are Aioli, made by adding fresh garlic, and Remoulàde, a gutsy sauce with vinegar, capers and shallots.

COUNTDOWN

Up to 2 days ahead
• Make mayonnaise and refrigerate.

INGREDIENTS

3 large egg yolks
4 tablespoons fresh lemon juice
   (1 large lemon)
1 teaspoon kosher salt

½ teaspoon ground white pepper
1 tablespoon Dijon mustard
1½ cups vegetable oil

In a food processor or blender, process egg yolks for one minute. Add lemon juice, salt, pepper and mustard and mix 1 more minute. With motor running, pour oil very slowly in a thin steady stream until half of it is added. Continue pouring a little faster until all the oil is absorbed and mayonnaise is thick and creamy. Refrigerate.

VARIATIONS:

AIOLI: When making mayonnaise, add 2 tablespoons minced garlic with the egg yolks.

REMOULÀDE SAUCE: To 1½ cups homemade mayonnaise, stir in:

INGREDIENTS

2 tablespoons drained capers
2 tablespoons minced parsley
1 teaspoon white wine vinegar
2 teaspoons finely chopped shallots

1 teaspoon Dijon mustard
Sea salt and freshly ground pepper
   to taste

MAKES 1½ CUPS

Huckleberry Sauce

COUNTDOWN

Up to 2 days ahead
• Make sauce and refrigerate.

The consistency of this vivid blue topping lies somewhere between a thin sauce and a thick syrup with the addition of softened berries. Besides Huckleberry Bread Pudding (page 60), use it on pancakes, waffles, ice cream, yogurt, sponge cakes, angel food cakes and shortcakes.

TIP:

• Wild fresh or frozen (do not defrost) blueberries make an excellent substitution for huckleberries.

INGREDIENTS

1 cup huckleberries	1 ½ teaspoons grated lemon peel
¼ cup sugar	1 ½ teaspoons lemon juice
¼ cup water	

Stir all ingredients together in a small saucepan. Simmer over very low heat for 15 to 20 minutes or until berries are very soft and liquid has become syrupy. Use at room temperature or chilled.

MAKES 1¼ CUPS

Spicy Peanut Sauce

COUNTDOWN

Up to 2 weeks ahead
• Make sauce and refrigerate. Serve at room temperature.

This sauce is delicious on Chinese Noodles with Grilled Chicken Breasts (page 52) and Grilled Pork Satay (page 46), but it's also great on roast chicken, roast pork and shrimp. You can even use it as a dip for fresh vegetables.

INGREDIENTS

½ cup vegetable oil	1 tablespoon coarsely chopped ginger
¼ cup tahini, stirred	½ cup crunchy regular peanut butter (not old fashioned)
¼ cup soy sauce	
2 tablespoons dry sherry	1 teaspoon dried red pepper flakes, or to taste
2 tablespoons rice vinegar	¼ cup water
½ teaspoon sesame oil	
⅓ cup honey	
1 tablespoon coarsely chopped garlic	

Place all ingredients in blender in order given and blend until pureed. Sauce can be served immediately or refrigerated. Serve at room temperature.

MAKES 2½ CUPS

Thai Red Curry Sauce

Thai red curry sauce is traditionally very spicy. I've toned down this version for the American palate by making it mildly spicy. You can vary the heat by increasing or decreasing the amount of jarred Thai red chili paste. Add it sparingly, a little at a time, until you obtain the heat you like. This versatile sauce is used for Grilled Tiger Prawn Satay (page 78) and Seared Alaskan Halibut (page 54).

(page 78) ... (page 54)

COUNTDOWN

Up to 2 weeks ahead
• Make sauce and refrigerate. Reheat before serving.

INGREDIENTS

2 tablespoons vegetable oil
¼ cup coarsely chopped lemongrass
¼ cup coarsely chopped galangal
2 tablespoons coarsely chopped garlic
2 tablespoons coarsely chopped shallots
1 cup aji-mirin

2 cans (13.5 ounces each) coconut milk, well stirred
2 tablespoons firmly packed Thai red curry paste
2 kaffir lime leaves
2 tablespoons Asian fish sauce (nuac mam)
1 tablespoon soy sauce

TO MAKE SAUCE: In a wok or 12-inch skillet, heat oil over high heat until almost smoking. Add lemongrass, galangal, garlic and shallots. Stir-fry for 2 minutes until aromatic. Add aji-mirin and cook, stirring, until reduced slightly, about 1 minute. Stir in coconut milk. Bring to a boil, reduce heat to medium-low and simmer for 20 minutes, or until thickened slightly. Add 2 tablespoons red curry paste, or to taste. Add lime leaves, stirring to break up paste. Bring to a boil over high heat, reduce heat to medium-low and simmer for 5 minutes. On low heat, stir in fish sauce and soy sauce. Strain sauce into a small bowl. Use immediately or refrigerate. Reheat before serving.

MAKES 2 CUPS

Tomato Sauce with Basil

Good quality roasted sun-dried tomatoes add a depth of flavor, but, unlike tomato paste, they help the sauce retain its light texture. Use this sauce on pasta, grilled or sautéed white fish, meatloaf and chicken breasts.

COUNTDOWN

Up to 6 hours ahead
• Make sauce and hold at room temperature. Serve warm or at room temperature.

INGREDIENTS

1 can (14 ounces) whole tomatoes in tomato juice
2 tablespoons olive oil
½ cup chopped onions
1 tablespoon finely chopped garlic

¼ cup whole roasted sun-dried tomatoes in olive oil, finely chopped
½ cup thinly julienned fresh basil
½ teaspoon sea salt
¼ teaspoon freshly ground pepper

TO MAKE SAUCE: Remove tomatoes to a medium bowl. Press with your hands to coarsely break them up. Add ½ cup of the tomato juice. Set aside. Put olive oil, onions and garlic into a large unheated skillet. Turn heat to medium and cook, stirring occasionally, until onions are translucent, about 4 minutes. Remove from heat and stir in tomatoes, sun-dried tomatoes, basil, salt and pepper. Before serving, if desired, reheat briefly until warm, but do not cook it.

MAKES 3¼ CUPS

Vanilla Bean Crème Anglaise

Crème anglaise is the French term for a rich custard sauce. Although it is made with the same ingredients as flan and other custards, this sauce is made on top of the stove. It is important to cook it over very low heat; the slower you cook it, the thicker it will become. Because the sauce can curdle if overheated, it is best to use either a candy or instant read thermometer. I serve it with Huckleberry Bread Pudding (page 60), but it is delicious on all types of desserts from fruits, to cakes, mousses and steamed puddings.

COUNTDOWN

Up to 2 days ahead
• Make sauce. Refrigerate in a covered container.

TIPS:

• The use of cornstarch in making crème anglaise is untraditional, but when cooking the custard, it helps keep it from curdling.

• If the sauce does curdle, use an immersion blender or put sauce into a blender.

INGREDIENTS

4 egg yolks
3 tablespoons sugar
Pinch of sea salt

1 teaspoon cornstarch
1½ cups milk
One 3-inch vanilla bean

TO PREPARE SAUCE: In a mixing bowl with electric mixer, beat yolks, sugar and salt until thick and light colored, about 3 minutes. Mix in cornstarch. Pour milk into a medium heavy saucepan. Slit vanilla bean down center and with the tip of a sharp knife, scrape seeds into milk. Add bean to milk. Scald over medium heat until small bubbles appear around the edges. Pour a little of the hot milk into yolks, mixing constantly. While mixing, slowly pour in remainder of milk. Return mixture to saucepan. Rinse out mixing bowl and set a fine-mesh strainer over the top. Using a heat-proof rubber spatula or wooden spoon, stir the sauce gently, but constantly, over low heat, making sure to reach the corners and bottom of the pan, 4 to 5 minutes. A thermometer should read 170°F. The sauce should be the consistency of heavy cream. Immediately pour custard through strainer. Set bowl in a bowl of ice water and stir occasionally until cool. Serve chilled.

MAKES 1½ CUPS

Wasabi-Orange Cream

This creamy sauce, flavored with wasabi and orange oil, enhances lumpia, spring rolls, egg rolls and sushi. It is also wonderful with steamed and grilled fish. An added bonus is that it takes only 5 minutes to prepare.

INGREDIENTS

1 cup mayonnaise

1 tablespoon orange oil

2 teaspoons wasabi paste, or to taste

TO PREPARE CREAM: In a medium bowl, whisk mayonnaise, orange oil and wasabi. For a spicier sauce, stir in more wasabi.

MAKES 1 CUP

COUNTDOWN

Up to 1 week ahead

• Make sauce and refrigerate. Bring to room temperature before serving.

Lobster bisque shoupers- soup served in a shot glass.

Garnishes

Crispy Fried Sage Leaves

Sage leaves are a tasty garnish for pasta, risotto and seafood.

INGREDIENTS

1 cup vegetable oil for frying

12 sage leaves, rinsed and dried

TO FRY LEAVES: In a small saucepan over medium heat, heat oil to 360°F. Drop 6 sage leaves, one at a time, into the oil. Fry for 20 to 30 seconds or until crisp. With a slotted spoon, remove to a plate lined with a double thickness of paper towels. Repeat with remaining leaves.

MAKES 12 LEAVES

COUNTDOWN

Up to 4 hours ahead
• Fry sage leaves and keep uncovered at room temperature.

Crispy Fried Shallots

When you are looking to dress up a dish with flavor and crunch, sprinkle these small fried shallot rings on top. They are terrific on vegetables, steaks, stews, salads and soups. But don't start sampling them – they are addictive.

COUNTDOWN

Up to 4 hours ahead
• Fry shallots and keep uncovered at room temperature.

TIPS:

• Choose the largest shallots you can find. They will be easier to slice and cook.

• For best results, slice the shallots on the thin setting of a mandoline.

• If you don't have a deep fat fryer, choose a saucepan that is about 9 inches wide and 3 inches deep. It is easier to fry in a shallow pan than a deep one.

INGREDIENTS

½ cup all-purpose flour

4 shallots, peeled and very
   thinly sliced

Vegetable oil for frying

TO FRY SHALLOTS: Place flour in a medium bowl. Add shallot slices and toss to coat. Put the floured shallots into a strainer and holding it over the sink, shake it gently to remove excess flour. The slices should be lightly coated. Fill a deep fat fryer with oil as directed or fill a wide saucepan with 2 inches of oil. Heat to 360°F on a deep fat or candy thermometer. Add about one-third of the shallots and cook, stirring with a skimmer for 45 seconds or until golden. Remove to a small bowl lined with a double thickness of paper towels. Repeat with remaining shallots, one-third at a time. Season with sea salt and pepper. Serve at room temperature.

Crispy Fried Spinach

I use fried spinach to garnish Lacquered Quail (page 100). It is so tasty and attractive that you can use it on almost anything.

INGREDIENTS

Vegetable oil for frying

Spinach leaves, rinsed and thoroughly dried

TO FRY SPINACH: In a small saucepan over medium heat, heat 2 to 3 inches of oil to 360°F. Drop 8 spinach leaves, one at a time, into the oil. Be careful, the water in the spinach can cause the oil to bubble up. If it does, cover with a lid for a few seconds. Fry for 60 to 90 seconds or until crisp. With a slotted spoon, remove to a plate lined with a double thickness of paper towels. Repeat with remaining spinach. Season with sea salt and pepper to taste.

COUNTDOWN

Up to 4 hours ahead
- Fry spinach and keep uncovered at room temperature.

Crispy Vegetable Chips

Move over potato chips, you have some stiff competition. At Va de Vi, we go through so many of these chips a day, I sometimes think I should open my own chip company.

TIPS:

- Use a mandoline to slice the vegetables about as thin as a dime.
- If possible, use Chinese taro.
- When working with taro, either wear rubber gloves or wash your hands as soon as possible. Taro contains an enzyme that reacts with the skin and makes it itch.

INGREDIENTS

Taro root, 1 to 1½ inches wide, peeled and thinly sliced

Parsnip, peeled and thinly sliced at an angle to get larger slices

Lotus root, peeled and thinly sliced

Vegetable oil for frying

Sea salt

TO PREPARE VEGETABLES: Put taro in a colander and rinse well. Put each type of sliced vegetable in a separate bowl and cover with water until ready to cook. Before frying, drain well and blot dry.

TO FRY TARO: In a deep fat fryer or Dutch oven, heat 3 to 4 inches of oil to 365°F. Add a few taro slices at a time and cook slowly in batches without crowding. Turn with tongs until they are crisp and edges are golden, 4 to 5 minutes. Remove to baking sheet lined with paper towels. Sprinkle with sea salt.

TO FRY PARSNIPS AND LOTUS: In a deep fat fryer or Dutch oven, heat 3 to 4 inches of oil to 365°F. Add a few parsnip and lotus slices and cook in batches without crowding. Turn with tongs until they are light golden, about 3 minutes. They will feel soft, but will firm up and turn darker as they cool. Remove to baking sheet lined with paper towels. Sprinkle with sea salt.

COUNTDOWN

Up to 4 hours ahead
- Soak vegetables in water.

Up to 3 hours ahead
- Fry vegetables and keep uncovered at room temperature.

Green Onion Curls

Here's a simple garnish for salads, soups and saucy meat dishes.

INGREDIENTS

2 green onions

TO PREPARE CURLS: Trim bottoms of onions, cut 2 inches off tops and remove outer layers. Using a sharp knife, cut stalks into thirds. Diagonally cut each into thin julienne slivers. Put them into a small bowl and cover with water. Refrigerate until they curl, at least 30 minutes. They can be stored in the refrigerator in water overnight, but I like to use them at room temperature when I garnish hot food.

COUNTDOWN

Up to 1 day ahead
- Prepare onions and refrigerate.

Pear and Star Anise Chutney

COUNTDOWN

Up to 3 days ahead
• Make chutney and refrigerate.

Fifteen minutes! That's all the time it takes to cook this sweet and spicy condiment.

INGREDIENTS

2 ripe pears, bosc preferred
2 star anise
⅓ cup unseasoned rice vinegar

1 tablespoon sugar
1 teaspoon fresh chopped thyme

Peel, core and chop pears into ¼-inch pieces. Put into a small saucepan. Add star anise, vinegar, sugar and thyme. Bring to a boil over medium heat. Boil slowly on medium-low for 10 minutes, stirring often, or until almost all the liquid is absorbed. Remove star anise and cool to room temperature. Use immediately or refrigerate. Bring to room temperature before serving.

MAKES 1 CUP

Pickled Cucumbers

COUNTDOWN

As far ahead as desired
• Make cucumbers and refrigerate indefinitely as long as they are submerged in the pickling solution.

These easy to make pickles are a great foil to spicy dishes. They are also terrific for snacking, or in salads and sandwiches.

INGREDIENTS

1 bottle (12 ounces) unseasoned
   rice vinegar
¾ cup superfine sugar

2 teaspoons sea salt
1 hot house English cucumber,
   very thinly sliced

In a bowl, stir together vinegar, sugar and salt. Stir in cucumbers. Make sure they are submerged in liquid. Refrigerate for at least 4 hours or until soft.

MAKES ABOUT 2½ CUPS

Pickled Onions

These easy to make onions are great on all types of salads. They also make a great addition to sandwiches. In the restaurant, I often pair them with smoked salmon and thin slices of cucumber.

COUNTDOWN

As far ahead as desired
• Onions may be refrigerated indefinitely as long as they are submerged in the pickling solution.

TIP:
• Onions may be sliced on a mandoline or by hand with a sharp knife.

INGREDIENTS

1 bottle (12 ounces) unseasoned rice vinegar
½ cup superfine sugar

1½ teaspoons kosher salt
1 red onion, thinly sliced

In a medium bowl, stir together vinegar, sugar and salt. Stir in onions. Make sure they are submerged in liquid. Cover and refrigerate overnight before using.

MAKES ABOUT 2 CUPS

Tempura Enoki

It is important to work with very cold batter when making tempura. The batter sticks better when it's cold and makes a crisper coating.

COUNTDOWN

Just before serving
• Make mushrooms.

TIP:
• Tempura batter can be used on all types of food, such as button, cremini and shiitake mushrooms, onion rings, zucchini and shrimp.

INGREDIENTS

Vegetable oil for frying
½ cup ice cubes
1 egg

½ cup plus 2 tablespoons flour
1 package (3.5 ounces) enoki mushrooms

In a deep fat fryer or small saucepan, heat 2 to 3 inches of oil to 360°F.

TO MAKE BATTER: Fill a 2 cup measure with ½ cup ice cubes. Add 1 egg and enough water to make 1 cup liquid. Stir with a fork until blended. Put flour into a medium bowl. Add the egg/ice mixture and stir with a fork until the mixture looks like pancake batter. It will be a little lumpy and have ice cubes in it.

TO FRY: Oil is ready when a few drops of batter sprinkled into it immediately float to the top. Pick up a small bunch of mushrooms with your hand. Holding them by the end of the stems, dip them into the batter until coated. Carefully add enoki to the hot oil, shaking them a little to separate. If they spatter, cover the pan with a lid for a few seconds. Fry, turning with tongs, until golden, about 2 minutes. Remove to a tray lined with paper towels. Season with sea salt and pepper to taste.

Glossary

AJI-MIRIN

A sweet rice wine used as a seasoning and sweetener in Japanese cuisine.

BOTTARGA DI MUGGINE

Bottarga is the salted, pressed and dried roe of the gray mullet (muggine). This delicacy is a specialty of the islands of Sardinia and Sicily. The mullet's eggs, after being extracted, are washed and purified, put under salt, rinsed and laid to dry. The aging process takes four to five months. Bottarga can be sliced, chopped, grated or shaved; a little goes a long way in adding delicious flavor to a dish.

CIPOLLINI ONIONS

These small, flat onions are very sweet with a delicate flavor. Select those that are firm and heavy for their size and have no dark spots. Cipollini have a dry, papery skin that must be peeled before using.

COCONUT MILK

Coconut milk is an essential part of Thai cooking that serves the same purpose as dairy cream in Western cuisines. It mellows other flavors in a dish, adds richness and smoothes textures.

Purchase it in cans marked 'unsweetened'. You do not want the sweet coconut cream used in pina coladas. Because the cream tends to rise to the top of the can, shake the can and open from the bottom. After the can is opened, the milk may be refrigerated for up to 2 days.

DEMI-GLACE

Also called glace de viande, this rich sauce is made by slowly cooking stock until it's reduced by half. The result is a thick glaze that coats a spoon and adds flavor and color to sauces. Many culinary shops sell it in paste or granulated form, which must be diluted in water. The purchased variety is weaker than homemade, so you must add the desired amount to taste.

EDAMAME

Edamame, a shell bean, is an immature green soybean. It is often called the wonder vegetable because it is the only vegetable that contains all nine essential amino acids, which makes it a complete source of protein. The popularity of this bean has grown in the past decade and is now found fresh or frozen in most major supermarkets.

FARRO

Farro, the original grain from which all others derive, fed the Mediterranean and Near Eastern populations for thousands of years. It has a firm, chewy texture that is delicious in hearty soups, stews and side dishes. The best grains are ¼ to ⅓ of an inch and labeled triticum dicoccum, farro's Latin name. Store it like any other grain, in a sealed glass container in a cool dry place.

FAVA BEANS

Tan fava beans resemble large lima beans. The first-of-the-season young beans are smaller, have tender skins, and don't need to be peeled after shelling. More mature, late beans need to be blanched to remove their tough, bitter outer skin before cooking.

FISH SAUCE

Known as nuac mam in Vietnam and nam pla in Thailand, it is used in those countries like soy sauce is used in China and Japan. A thin, brown liquid made from fermented shrimp or fish, it has a salty, pungent flavor which cannot be duplicated.

FUKUJIN ZUKE

This popular Japanese condiment is made from finely chopped daikon, eggplant, cucumbers and other vegetables, pickled in soy.

FURIKAKE, FUMI FURIKAKE, NORI FUMI FURIKAKE

Furikake is a blend of spices and ingredients that is often used as a seasoning for rice. There are many different varieties, but it usually consists of toasted nori (seaweed), sesame seeds, bonito (dried tuna) flakes, sugar and salt.

GALANGAL

A root with culinary and medicinal uses that grows throughout Southeast Asia. It resembles ginger in appearance and taste, but has an extra citrus and distinct earthy aroma of its own.

GREEN GARLIC

Young garlic, which resembles a green onion, is used before it begins to form cloves. It has a long, green stalk and a white root end that is sometimes tinged with pink. Its flavor is milder than mature garlic.

KAFIR (KAFFIR) LIME LEAVES

The leaves from a dark-green knobby lime are so aromatic, their flavor has no substitute. Usually found frozen, use what you need and return any remaining to the freezer. If fresh, tear them in half and pull off their coarse center veins before using.

LEMONGRASS

This tall, hard grayish-green grass is used for its citrus aroma and flavor in much of Southeast Asian cooking. It is sold by the stalk, which is about 2 feet in length. It is fibrous to the point of being woody. For this reason it is valued for the flavor it imparts. Store with the bottom end in a little water to keep it from drying out. The peel of a quarter of a lemon may be substituted.

LUMPIA, LUMPIA WRAPPER

Called egg rolls in America and lumpia in Indonesia and the Philippines, they are part of the spring roll family based in China. Lumpia is made with ground or finely chopped food that is wrapped in a very thin wrapper made of flour, water and sometimes an egg and usually fried. Lumpia wraps come either square or round, refrigerated or frozen. The refrigerated, square ones are the easiest to work with. Menlo and Simex are the preferred brands.

MIREPOIX

This is a mixture of diced carrots, onions, celery and herbs used to season sauces, soups and stews. It is also used as a bed on which to braise meats and fish.

OCEAN OR SEAWEED SALAD

This popular Japanese salad is normally made from wakame seaweed, agar-agar (a vegetable 'gelatin' derived from a number of seaweeds), sesame oil, kikurage mushrooms and sesame seed.

PANKO

These bread crumbs are used in Japanese cooking to coat fried foods. Lighter and coarser than regular bread crumbs, panko create a beautiful, crunchy crisp crust.

RED CURRY PASTE

This paste is a complex, fiery Thai mixture containing at least a dozen spices, including chilies, garlic, onion, kafir lime leaves, galangal, cumin, turmeric and others. Even in Thailand, cooks purchase ready-made curry pastes instead of making their own. There are many different kinds of curry paste; green and yellow are even hotter than the red. It is often combined with coconut milk to make curries and sauces.

SHICHIMI TOGARASHI, NANAMI TOGARASHI OR SICHIMI TOGARASHI

Known as Japanese seven-spice, togarashi is the Japanese word for red chili peppers. It is also the generic name for a family of condiments that blend chili pepper with other ingredients. The exact spices vary, but most often include powdered red chili pepper, black pepper, sesame seeds, dried mandarin orange peel, green nori (seaweed) flakes, sansho (a Japanese pepper berry), hemp seeds and poppy seeds.

SHISO

An herb from the perilla plant, shiso looks like a jagged-edged leaf and tastes like a combination of basil and mint. There are red and green varieties, but the green is more commonly used in salads, sushi, sashimi and garnishes.

SRIRACHA SAUCE

A commercial, all-purpose Thai chili sauce that resembles an orange-red catsup. It is used in cooking and as a condiment and is available in hot or mild forms.

STAR ANISE

This flower or star-shaped brownish-black pod is native to China. It has a pronounced anise flavor that is slightly more pungent than regular anise seeds.

THAI BASIL

This aromatic herb is also called holy basil, because it is a sacred herb in India. It is a very common ingredient in Thai cuisine for flavoring curries and stir-fries. It has a strong flavor similar to anise seed. Ordinary basil and fresh mint are the best substitutes.

WASABI

Known as Japanese horseradish, wasabi is a perennial herb that comes from the root of an Asian plant. It is not related to horseradish, but resembles it with its strong, hot flavor. Pale green in color, it is widely available in the U.S. in paste and powder form. The powder must be mixed with water to create a paste.

WASABI TOBIKO

This flying fish roe is flavored with wasabi, which gives it a pale or bright green hue.

Techniques

GRATING GINGER

To finely grate ginger, peel a knob of ginger, but leave it attached to the larger knob. This will give you something to hold onto. Grate on a Microplane or the finest holes of a grater.

PEELING AND DEVEINING SHRIMP

It is better to peel shrimp yourself because pre-peeled shrimp have lost some of their flavor. To peel them, hold the shrimp in one hand, grab the legs with the other hand and pull them off. With your fingers, peel away the outer shell. To remove the tail portion, pinch the shell to break it and gently tug it off. The vein of a shrimp is actually its intestinal tract and can impart a bitter taste. To remove the vein, hold the peeled shrimp in one hand with its back facing you. With a paring knife, make a shallow incision down the length of the back and remove the vein with the tip of the knife, then rinse the shrimp.

TOASTING SESAME SEEDS

Heat a small skillet, preferably cast iron, over medium-low heat. Add 2 to 3 tablespoons sesame seeds. Stir until they turn a shade darker and give off a roasted aroma. If they fly around as you are stirring, either turn down the heat or cover the pan loosely. Toasted sesame seeds may be stored in a tightly closed jar for several weeks.

STORING HERBS

For basil, snip a tiny slice off the bottom of the stems. Put the stems in a jar of water like you would flowers and keep it at room temperature. Change the water every other day. The basil will last for several days, sometimes weeks and often it will begin to flower.

For parsley, mint and other herbs with soft stems, put into a container of water like you would flowers. Cover them loosely with a plastic bag and store in the refrigerator. Change the water every 2 to 3 days. They will stay fresh for several days and sometimes weeks.

STORING GREEN ONIONS

Wrap in damp paper towels and put them into a plastic bag. Seal the bag and store in a vegetable drawer.

CHOPPING LEMONGRASS

First trim off the top and outer layers of leaves. Only the bulb-like 6-to 8-inches of the stalk is used. In order to release its flavor, pound the stalk with a hammer or back of a cleaver to break up the fibers. To chop, first cut off the hard knot at the end, then slice crossways into thin slices and chop.

BOILING EGGS

Put eggs into a pan and cover with cold water by half an inch. Bring to a full boil. Cover, remove from heat and let sit 15 minutes. Drain and immediately put them into a bowl of ice water. This eliminates the ring around the yolk. Peel under cold running water by first tapping the wide end of the shell, which has an air pocket.

CUTTING CORN OFF THE COB

Remove the husk and silk from an ear of corn. Stand the ear in a bowl, holding it by its stem. Slide a small, sharp knife down the length of the cob, slicing the kernels off into the bowl, being careful not to cut into the cob. Rotate the ear until all the kernels are off. For creamier corn, press the back of the knife against the cob and rub it lengthwise to remove the juices and milk, rotating around the cob.

STORING AND CLEANING MUSHROOMS

Wrap unwashed mushrooms loosely in damp paper towels or in a loosely closed paper bag. Leave packaged mushrooms in their unopened package. Clean mushrooms with a soft brush or wipe with a damp paper towel. If the mushrooms are very gritty, rinse them quickly under cold running water and pat dry. Oyster are the cleanest of all the mushrooms, so they do not need rinsing. To use, gently pull them apart with your fingers.

Don't soak mushrooms, because their delicate tissues absorb water. If desired, slice ¼ inch off the bottom of the stems to refresh them. If only caps are called for in a recipe, cut the stem flush with the cap.

DEEP FRYING

There are a few simple rules for deep fat frying. It is easiest and safest done in an electric deep fat fryer, because it is important for the oil to maintain an even temperature. If you don't have an electric fryer, fill a wok, electric skillet or saucepan with at least 2 to 3 inches of vegetable oil. You need to have enough oil so that the food does not touch the bottom of the pan. It is extremely helpful to attach a thermometer to the pan. For best results, fry food in batches, without crowding. Use a wire-mesh strainer or large holed scoop to remove as many pieces as possible at one time and shake gently over pan to allow oil to drip back in. Do not use a slotted spoon because it does not drain adequately. Spread the food in a single layer on paper towels. When the oil has cooled, it can be strained through a double mesh strainer into a bowl or jar, covered and stored in a cool, dark place. The oil can be reused once or twice, if it was not used for frying fish.

Index

06/05/05 here and
First time here.
it was a great time.
Love the variety
in each dish
and want dinner(?)
with any of them
Thanks for a great dinner!
—Mmm...

June 12, 2005
What a wonderful
afternoon — it felt
very decadent — the
service, wine, food + atmosphere
were all — fantastic!
We'll be back!!

Isabella Bautista

="09" GHanna Wirth

6/19/05 Hula Girls
The have been
here
wanna
picture?
$5

GREAT!!
FOOD
& WINE!